# Don't let an **Old Person** *move into* **YOUR BODY**

# Don't let an
# Old Person
## *move into*
# YOUR
# BODY

How to Make
the Rest of
Your Life,
the Best of
Your Life

## JIM DONOVAN

TO ALBERT

Cover design by Genevieve LaVo Cosdon
www.lavodesign.com

Copy editing by Donna Eliassen, Viking Virtual Services
www.a1vikingvirtualservices.com

AUSTIN BAY
POST OFFICE BOX 63
UPPER BLACK EDDY, PA 18972

www.JimDonovan.com

ISBN:978-0-97868916-2

Library of Congress Control Number: 2009928947

*Printed in the United States of America*

*Dedicated to Georgia, my wife and best friend. Without her patience, support and encouragement, this book would never have been written.*

# CONTENTS

Acknowledgments _____ v

Introduction_____ vii

1. Challenging the Myths _____ 1

2. Redefining Your Purpose and Reigniting Your Passion_____ 15

3. Creating Your Compelling Vision _____ 33

4. Whatsoever You Believe_____ 49

5. Attitude Is Everything_____ 67

6. If You Don't Have Your Health, All Bets Are Off _____ 87

7. You Don't Have to Eat Dog Food _____ 123

8. Simple Steps to Enhance Your Life _____ 141

9. The Best of Your Life _____ 161

Bonus Gifts_____ 163

About the Author_____ 164

Additional Resources _____ 166

Reading List_____ 168

# ACKNOWLEDGEMENTS

To my mother, Marguerite Donovan, for teaching me to read and encouraging me in whatever I did, no matter how absurd it seemed at the time.

Special thanks to Genevieve LaVo Cosdon for making the design process fun and for designing an awesome book cover.

Thanks to Donna Eliassen for lending her talent and eye for copy editing, Tracy Ivie for her copywriting help with the cover copy, and Denise Adelsberger for her administrative assistance.

Thanks to Monika Kovacs for her fitness and exercise suggestions.

My friend and mastermind partner Art (Ski) Swiatkowski for keeping me on track and moving in the right direction.

Jim Sutton for being my friend and for being in my corner throughout it all. You are the best.

Thanks and appreciation to Suzanne Somers for having the courage to publish breakthrough ideas for living a vibrant life.

And to Bill Faloon and the Life Extension Foundation for educating me about the latest advances in alternative medicine.

Special thanks to all those *ageless* people who taught me that aging does not mean getting old and that you can be who you want to be and do what you want to do, no matter what your age.

Lastly, I want to thank all the people who have read my previous books, for providing me with encouragement and inspiration throughout the years. I am honored to have been a part of your lives.

# INTRODUCTION

*"While being young is an accident of time,
youth is a permanent state of mind"*
FRANK LLOYD WRIGHT

Have you ever noticed that some people age well, becoming older with grace and dignity, looking vibrant and alive and remaining physically and mentally active well into old age? Frank Lloyd Wright, quoted above, was still designing when he passed on at 92.

Others, it seems, begin getting old in their youth. What makes the difference?

Why is such a large portion of our society aging so poorly? Why are hospitals and nursing homes overcrowded and many older people just barely alive?

Is this a natural progression or can we actually alter the way we age?

The Bible teaches us that we have a natural life expectancy of 120 – 150 years. Many of the people written about in the Old Testament lived to be over one hundred, and in some

parts of the world today, entire villages live well beyond one
hundred years of age.

## It's not how long you live; it's how you live long

What are the secrets of a long and productive life and what
can you do about it? More importantly, how can you live your
life to the fullest, enjoying an abundance of health, wealth,
and happiness? How can you make the most of your life, for
however long you are here?

How can you live, laugh, and love more? What steps can
you take, starting now, to achieve the best level of health and
fitness you are capable of reaching? How can you get back in
touch with your dreams and desires and begin to experience
them? How can you learn to age with passion, purpose,
power, and prosperity?

In *Don't Let an Old Person Move Into Your Body,* you will be
asked to reevaluate and question the preconceived notions
you have about aging and the commonly accepted beliefs
about health. You will be asked to examine your attitudes and
beliefs and come to understand the important role they play
in how we age. You will learn ways to age without becoming
old.

You'll be introduced to people who have aged successfully
and learn their strategies. You will learn about the latest
developments in the field of longevity and identify ways you
can minimize, even slow, the process of aging. You will create

a compelling vision for your future and a plan for a long, active, and prosperous life.

I invite you to join me in this exciting journey into aging and learn how you, too, can develop your personal plan of aging with passion, purpose, power and prosperity, and make sure you don't let an old person move into *your* body.

It is your God-given birthright to have a life of joy, happiness, health, love, fun, prosperity, excitement, abundance, and all the other wonderful things life on earth has to offer. To accept less is to shortchange yourself and your loved ones.

*Don't Let an Old Person Move Into Your Body* has been developed from the work that I have done in live seminars and workshops as well as with individual clients. I ask that you, my friend, approach reading this as if you were with me at a live event. You will be asked, from time to time, to stop reading and complete action steps or write in your journal. Please complete the simple actions as they have been

> *Within you is the power to change your life.*
>
> — JIM DONOVAN

created to help you design a future that will enable you to make the rest of your life, the best of your life.

As with any book, do not simply accept what is written. Test it for yourself and take from it only that which feels right for you. After all, this is your life.

Please keep in mind, throughout this book, that within you

is the power to change your life.

Before we begin, I'd like you to think about your intention for reading this book. Intentions are very powerful. They send our desires out into the universe.

Stop reading for a moment and think about why you are reading this book. What do you want to take from the experience? In my live seminars, I ask people to share why they're attending and what they intend to take from our time together. Obviously, I cannot do that with you, but I can ask you to think about what your response would be.

Do you intend to simply read the book or do you want more? Do you intend to take the ideas presented here, integrate them into your day-to-day life and use them to create an exciting and compelling future?

If you have read any of my other books, you know I don't write about theory. I write from my own experiences. I know with absolute certainty that the principles, techniques and ideas presented here work, because I have used them to change my own life from one of misery and depression, to living today what I can only describe as a truly magical life. I continue to apply these principles daily as my own life continues to expand and I enjoy even more of the joy and beauty that surrounds us.

I am truly blessed. When I pass a homeless person on the street, I always say a prayer for the unfortunate person as well as a prayer of gratitude, for I understand deeply the phrase

"There but for the grace of God, go I."

I have lived in depression and, at more than one point in my life, I was without a place to call home. I have been at the bottom, gone without food for days at a time, lived in poverty, and sold most of my possessions. I once heard the motivational speaker, Anthony Robbins, talk about washing dishes in the bathtub because the room where he lived had no sink and I laughed because I had done that too.

I've slept in cars and spent endless hours sitting on park benches for lack of anywhere else to go. I've walked the streets of New York City, hoping to find enough loose change to buy a pack of cigarettes, which gave new meaning to the phrase, "I'd walk a mile for a Camel."

I do not share these stories to gain your sympathy, for it was all a result of my own doing. I do not share this to be unique for there are many people whose lives have experienced more pain than I can ever imagine. I share this with you, my friend, so that you will understand that no matter where you are right now, you have within you the power to create the life you were born to live.

Today when I awaken each morning, before I get out of bed, I say a short prayer that I learned from the Reverend Robert Schuller, "This is the day which the Lord hath made. We will rejoice and be glad in it," for I know today that my life is a gift and no matter what happens, I am living a life beyond my wildest dreams.

My life today is magical. I have a loving wife, abundant health and a wonderful home in one of the most beautiful parts of the United States. I am surrounded by nature. And I have all the material possessions that I could possibly want, but more importantly, my life has purpose. I am privileged to spend my time writing books and being able to share what I have learned with others.

My books have been sold throughout the world and I am fortunate to have been able to touch the lives of many, many people in a positive way.

I get to speak to groups of people and share my message so that others may use these ideas in their own life. The biggest thrill for me today is seeing the sparkle in a person's eye, when they too realize that they can, in fact, create the life that they were born to live.

I know that as you read this book and complete the action steps, you will reach that point when your eyes sparkle, for you will have connected with the ideas presented here and will have made them your own. You will have claimed your personal power and begun designing your life the way you want it to be.

So if you're ready, let's begin the journey to make the rest of your life the best of your life.

# 1

# CHALLENGING THE MYTHS

**Myth #1**

*"You're getting on in years — you'd better slow down."*
*"At my age, I'd better be careful."*
*"Act your age!"*
*"We'll all wind-up in a nursing home sooner or later."*
*"The older you get, the more medication you'll need."*
*"I'm just having a senior moment."*

All of the above statements are nonsense. There's no biological connection between age and poor health. We don't have to deteriorate as we get older. I first witnessed the principle of healthy aging in action many years ago, while living in La Jolla,

California, a beautiful town nestled along the Pacific coast just north of San Diego.

The Southern California coast, with its awesome beauty and mild climate, is conducive to outdoor activity and it is not unusual to see people of all ages engaged in some kind of physical activity. There was a saying that, "If you were able to turn 360 degrees and not see at least three different sports being played, you were not in San Diego."

La Jolla has a lovely cove where people swim and scuba dive. One sunny morning I was taking a walk through the La Jolla Park. Passing by the cove, I noticed a group of people about to take a swim. As I came closer, I saw that they were older people, well into their 80's and beyond and that they were going to swim out to the big rock that sits out about a half a mile from the shore.

It was then that I realized there are other ways to age besides the slow deterioration we have been taught is our fate. These elderly folks were going to swim over a mile — in the ocean of all places! At the time I thought to myself, "If I tried that I'd probably drown." Although a lot younger, I was in no shape to be swimming that distance.

These people were very old. Some looked to be 90, yet all were in top physical condition and appeared to be quite healthy. I later learned that this swim was something these aging seniors did on a regular basis.

The lesson I learned that day stayed with me and greatly

influenced my beliefs about aging and the possibility of growing older without giving up our health and mobility.

## My role model for aging

While I never had the pleasure of actually meeting him, Mr. Eli Finn became my role model for positive aging many years ago, years before I even considered writing this book. Eli was a close friend of my wife's aunt, Josie Ferrone, herself an aging woman, in her late eighties at the time.

Aunt Josie, however, remained quite active for most of her life. If you wanted to call her, you had better do it early in the day because chances are she had plans to attend a luncheon or go to the theater. At 83, she still commuted part-time from her home in Fairfield, Connecticut to New York City where she worked as a bookkeeper for an AFL-CIO union. At one time Josie had even met and spoken with Mrs. Eleanor Roosevelt.

Aunt Josie's affirmation was, "Every day above ground is a good day." It served her well until her passing at age 96. Aunt Josie had met Eli Finn when they were both commuting to New York. He had worked as a salesperson for a company in Harlem and traveled daily from his home in Norwalk until his retirement at 100 years of age.

Being bored with so much time on his hands, and wanting to remain active, he enrolled in college as a full-time student and remained active and vibrant until his passing, from natural causes, at 107. Well past the century mark, Eli was still vacationing to

Europe, tending his garden, and living his life to the fullest.

When asked about his longevity, he replied simply, "Be involved and have a good attitude."

It saddens me when I see older people using canes and walkers, especially since I know, in many cases, it could have been prevented. With the exception of accidents and injuries, the crippling effects of aging we see are the result of poor health choices, a sedentary lifestyle, lack of exercise and most of all, the acceptance that this is a "normal" part of the aging process. It is not. This will become quite clear as you read in Chapter 8 what the various health authorities have to say.

It saddens me how quickly people will accept the stereotypes of aging without the slightest question. I have some friends, for example, who are somewhat older than I and it astounds me how nonchalantly they say things like, "I better slow down, I'm not getting any younger you know." My late mother-in-law use to say, "It's tough getting old." In an effort to shift her focus, I would remind her that the alternative, not getting old, was worse.

I recently had an occasion to have a medical technician visit my home to conduct a routine insurance physical. It happened to occur just days after I hurt my back, a rare occasion in itself, and I was still having trouble standing upright. Without even asking she commented, "Oh, it's arthritis, it's just part of getting older, I have the same problems." How quickly we are to accept illness as a normal part of aging. This is nonsense.

4

If you interview a cross section of active older people you will soon begin to notice several characteristics they all share. In the coming pages, I will explore these characteristics in greater detail and offer some suggestions for how we can adapt their behaviors in our lives in order to live more fully as we age.

Something shared by many active people in their 80's and 90's and even older is that they continue to be engaged in careers that they enjoy or other activities that keep them occupied and enable them to make a contribution. They are engaged in volunteer work, a part-time endeavor, or even self-employment.

I'll always remember Frank Krause, a former client of mine. When I first met Mr. Krause, I always addressed him that way, not so much because he cared but because it always seemed appropriate. He was in his early 80's and was the owner of two businesses.

One day we drove in his car into the heart of New York City to look at some trade show displays. I had been working with him to develop a trade show booth for one of his companies. When he parked the car at 53rd Street and 6th Avenue, I grabbed my briefcase and jumped out so that I could help him out of the car.

After all, he was over 80!

But when I got out and looked around for him, he was gone! He was already a half a block down the street. I had to practically run to keep up with him. I realized right then and there that his boundless energy was in part due to his love for his business and the fact that it gave him challenging experiences to look forward to each day.

He also exercised several times a week, and of course, ate sensibly, but it was his love for his work and the companies he'd built that left him feeling connected and provided his "joie de vivre."

## Myth #2

*"Work hard, save your money, and when you retire you'll be able to finally enjoy your life."*

Bull! Nonsense! No! No way! Nein! Nyet! Aniyo! Iie! Non! If there was ever a misguided message given to people, this is it. Look at the absurdity of what we are told to believe and follow. You spend 25 or 30 years working in a job that you may or may not enjoy and save your money so that "someday" you can retire. While saving is sound advice, too many people take it to an extreme, depriving themselves of life's pleasures so they can squirrel away every cent to be enjoyed sometime in the future, which they may or may not ever live to see.

We are then told to put up with all this so we can "enjoy our retirement," which for many people who unknowingly bought in to this plan, means living on meager savings and social security. Is this living? I don't think so.

The very idea of retirement is flawed at its core. For one

thing, it establishes that a time will come when you are of no monetary value to society and will not be able to earn a living so you better be prepared. The sad truth is that many older citizens, due to the advances of medicine, are outliving their savings and have to rely on family to support them. In 2009, the Senior Citizens League estimated that five million seiors were living below the poverty line! I am a big believer in taking care of one's family, however, I also feel that we should be able and are entitled to support ourselves in the lifestyle of our choice.

One of the saddest things I've ever experienced was watching my father, in his twilight years, sit idly waiting for the mail to arrive each day. This was what his life had become.

### There are better role models for a better way to age.

Harland Sanders, best remembered for starting Kentucky Fried Chicken, now KFC, was 65 years old when he began his business. The story is that when he looked at his Social Security check of $105 a month, he realized he did not want to try to live on it alone. Until he died in 1980 at the age of 90, the Colonel traveled 250,000 miles a year visiting his KFC restaurants around the world.

On July 24, 1987, Hulda Crooks became the oldest person to climb Mt. Fuji in Japan. She was 91 years old at the time. Upon doing so, she exclaimed, "You always feel good when you make a goal."

Ray Kroc, a mixer salesman, met the McDonald brothers

and began his fast food empire when he was well into mid-life. He noted later, "I was 52 years old. I had diabetes and incipient arthritis. I had lost my gall bladder and most of my thyroid gland in earlier campaigns, but I was convinced that the best was ahead of me." Even with his health challenges, he remained active in his business and lived to be 82. Today, there are over 24,500 McDonald's restaurants in 115 countries.

Buckminster Fuller, bankrupt at 32 years old, went on to receive international recognition for his geodesic dome as he approached 60. And in 1970, he received the Gold Medal award from the American Institute of Architects at age 75. "Bucky" is rumored to have said, "Man doesn't even get good until he's 80!"

> *Man doesn't even get good until he's 80.*
>
> — BUCKMINSTER FULLER

Aside from the financial side of the retirement equation, and perhaps more important, is the issue of losing our sense of purpose. While our work is certainly not all that defines who we are, it is essential for us to feel that we are making some contribution to society. We need to feel as though we are "in the game" and not just sitting on the sidelines, watching life go by.

This became painfully apparent to me while visiting my mother in Melbourne, Florida one Christmas. In a department store doing some last minute shopping, I was about to get in line to pay for my purchase, when I noticed an older couple moving in the same direction and motioned for the man to go ahead of me. He looked at me and said, "No, you go ahead. I'm retired. I have nothing better to do." I vowed, then and there, to never let my life be reduced to a situation where standing in line in a department store was the high point of my day.

I'll always remember an experience I had while still in my twenties. My company was producing an audio training program for people nearing retirement, and as the producer, I was asked to attend the live seminars, one day a week for seven weeks. It was quite a unique experience for me, a 28-year old, to be part of a seminar with a bunch of people about to retire.

For the first two hours, I was simply an observer. Then, after a while, the group brought me into the discussion and I became a full participant. The lessons I learned in those weeks have stayed with me and contributed immensely to my opinions about aging and retirement.

At lunch on the first day of the seminar, I was sitting with a man named Bill, a Boston police officer about to retire after many years of service. When I asked him how he felt about this, he replied, "Lousy. I'm only 54, but because my job involves carrying a weapon, I have to retire. I don't know what I'm going to do with myself."

Up until that point, I thought the primary concern people

had was financial security. Was I ever wrong! While finances are very important, I realized that the bigger issue was what to do with the 10 to 12 hours each day that were not going to be taken up by working. Another concern that surfaced later in the program was the feeling that they had, somehow, lost their purpose in life.

Fortunately, the program was effective, and by the last week, the issue had been addressed. At the luncheon on the final day, I asked Bill how he now felt and what his plans were. His eyes lit up as he told me he planned on using his experience as a mounted policeman to teach horseback riding at a local academy part time and that he would finally have time to spend in his garden. Clearly, Bill was well on his way to a new, more exciting, adventure.

> *Here's a test to find out whether your mission on earth is finished; if you're alive, it isn't.*
>
> — RICHARD BACH

Many years ago, a friend of mind defined purpose as "a reason to expend energy." Purpose gives us a reason to get out of bed in the morning. It keeps us going in the face of adversity. It gives us the inner strength we need to overcome any obstacle. If your purpose or goal is strong enough, you will find a way. Our goals help us to answer the question, "Why am I doing this"?

Richard Bach, while best known for his classic book,

*Jonathan Livingston Seagull,* wrote another book *Illusions,* which is my personal favorite. It is the story of a bi-plane pilot who, in his travels, meets a master teacher. In one chapter he writes, "Here's a test to find out whether your mission on earth is finished; if you're alive, it isn't."

When I first read that statement, I was in my twenties and thought it quite profound. Now, years later, it holds even more meaning for me, and hopefully, for you. Since you're reading this book, I can safely assume you are still among the living. In this case, you are not yet done with your work here. The simple fact that you are here is proof that there is something else you have left to do, learn, or become.

Too many people see retirement as the end of their purpose in life. If you still have a pulse, you can do anything you want.

Now, let's get about the business of finding out what that might be.

## Living a balanced life

A good way to begin any personal growth program is by taking a close look at the different areas of your life. If you were buying a business, the first thing you would do is assess its current state of affairs. You would take inventory and examine the merchandise to determine what to keep and what to discard. You would examine the assets and take a look at the liabilities in order to know what to change.

You will do the same with your life. It is important to view your life in its entirety. To live a full and happy life requires balance in several areas. One of the challenges in our busy world today is maintaining that balance.

Our tendency is to become focused on one area, like money or career, and neglect others such as health or relationships. This can be devastating. You don't want to wind up with a lot of money at the expense of your family or health, do you? On the other hand, you don't want to be in great health but broke and homeless, without anyone who cares for you. It is important, when doing personal growth work, to maintain a balance and devote time and attention to each of the key areas that result in a fulfilling life.

## Action step — Personal inventory

Following are the areas you will want to include in your inventory. For each of these, closely examine your life at the present time. Where are your strengths? What areas could use some improvement immediately? Choose one or two and set some immediate goals to begin work in those areas.

For example, if you have identified health and fitness as an area you'd like to improve, you may want to begin by making an appointment for a complete physical check-up or sign up for the yoga class you've been meaning to take. It is these simple first steps that give us the motivation and momentum to continue making positive changes.

Later, you will complete a powerful visioning activity that

will incorporate each of these key areas, but for now, simply identify some things you could begin working on immediately.

- *Religion & Spirituality*
- *Self–development*
- *Health and Fitness*
- *Family and Relationships*
- *Career and Business*
- *Social and Material*
- *Money and Investments*

Please pause here and complete the activity above.

When you are ready to proceed, turn the page and let's take a closer look at purpose and how it relates to having a happy, fulfilling life.

# 2

## REDEFINING YOUR PURPOSE AND
## REIGNITING YOUR PASSION

*"Life is a daring adventure or nothing"*
HELEN KELLER

Comedians Bob Hope and George Burns talked about living to be 100 all throughout their lives. For someone of their generation, born in the 1800's, this was quit a feat. They also, by no coincidence continued to perform well into their 90's. I'll always remember Burns being asked by a reporter if it was true he was scheduled to perform at Caesar's Palace in Las Vegas for his 100th birthday. Burns, known for his quick, wit replied, "Yes, and I hope Caesar's is still in business by then." It never occurred to him that he would not live to fulfill his dream. As it turned out, although he was still living to see his 100th birthday, he was sick with the flu and was not able to perform.

The amazing thing here is that both men, who throughout their lives affirmed living to be 100 passed away within 90 days after their centennial celebration. I believe that what kept them alive and vibrant at ages that were decades past when most of their contemporaries lived, was their strong sense of purpose and love for their work.

In my first book, *Handbook to a Happier Life*, I retold a story about a priest who was advised by his doctor to go home and put his affairs in order because his illness was terminal and he did not have long to live. The priest's big dream was to visit a particular church in Peru before he passed, so off he went. As he was walking out of the church he saw a young boy running away with the poor box. He grabbed the boy by the back of his shirt and asked how dare he steal from the church. "I'm sorry Father," the boy replied, "But my friends and I are orphans and we're starving. I was just taking the money to buy food for us."

Not quite believing the lad, the priest asked to see where these so called starving children were. Taking the priest by the hand, the boy led him to where they were hiding. The priest, forgetting about his own problems, decided he had to do something. He began an orphanage to help the children, and some 25 years later, was still running it.

Andrew Carnegie, one of the most successful people of his

generation, taught that having a definite major purpose in life was one of the traits that was absolutely essential for success. Purpose is what gets us out of bed in the morning, raring to get going with our day.

Virtually all of the older people that I know or have read about, who are living vibrantly and appear happy, are engaged in some activity that brings them joy and personal satisfaction. They are not filling their days by pretending to be busy. The most alive people in our society are also, by no small coincidence, the most active and are usually engaged in a profession that gives them such joy that they

> *Find something that you are absolutely passionate about doing and do it.*

can not even consider not doing it. To me this is the big secret to success in life. Find something that you are absolutely passionate about doing, something that you can not imagine not doing, and do it. It could be anything from an artistic endeavor, a business, a career, or some other area of life.

In this chapter we will look at what some older people are doing and explore ways in which you might uncover your definite major purpose, whatever it may be. Please don't misunderstand; I am not suggesting this has to be work or a job. As a matter of fact, as far as I am concerned, if it feels like work, it's not really your purpose.

17

I am fortunate that years after what one reporter termed "aimless wandering," I uncovered something that brings me such satisfaction that I can not imagine not doing it. I recently gave a keynote talk at a high school graduation and told the graduates the secret to a successful life was to find something that you absolutely love to do and figure out a way to get paid for it.

It's interesting that while the adults in the audience laughed, the young people got it. Here are some people who found their purpose and are living it.

## They lived their passion

In 2001 Nina Bourne, VP and Director of Advertising at Knopf Publishing took a break from her daily tasks to celebrate her 85th birthday and then went right back to work.

Bernie Bahr retired from his traditional job and at 63 became a male stripper. One 50 year old fan said, "He shows you that you don't have to be 20 to be sexy!"

Author Phyliss Whitney, who passed away in 2008 at the age of 104, said in an Associated Press interview when she was 85 that "I've slowed down in that I only write one book a year. A writer is what I am." Her last novel, *Amethyst Dreams*, was published in 1997, and at 102, she began working on her autobiography. During her long and successful career she wrote more than 75 books and about a hundred short stories.

Wanting to make it easier for women to register to vote,

Doris Haddock, at 94, was leading a voter registration team travelling the US.

Elliott Carter, who turned 100 in 2008, won his second Pulitzer Prize for Music at age 65 for his String Quartet no.3 and his first Grammy award at 86 for a violin concerto. Then at 90, he turned to a new genre, opera, receiving rave reviews in the *Boston Globe* for his operatic work, *What's Next?*

Eleanor Lombard, called the "Empress of Fashion" for her part in promoting American fashions to the level of international respectability, worked in her office until she was 99 and then after closing it, still kept a few clients right up until her death at 100. Her work furthered the careers of big name designers like Bill Blass, Anne Klein, and Oscar De La Renta. Clearly, she had found her purpose and passion.

In 2006, Oleg Cassini was renovating a Manhattan town house to be a showcase for his collections when he died, at the age of 92.

## Play *your* special music

When a person is living their true purpose, their calling if you will, it's obvious. You may remember seeing the 1980 Olympics. I'll never forget the last scene at the closing ceremony, with Chuck Mangione conducting the orchestra in a great rendition of his hit song *Feels So Good*.

You could see the absolute joy Mangione was feeling as he literally jumped around, his arms in the air and a look of pure exuberance on his face. It was obvious that he was doing something that gave him great pleasure. Something he was born to do.

One of my favorite quotations is one from Ralph Waldo Emerson who said, "Most men (and women) die with their music still in them." While this is not a very uplifting statement, it serves to remind me to live my dreams and has become a driving force behind the work that I do. A big part of my purpose, my mission, is to do whatever I can to encourage people to live their dreams and play their special music. I believe each of us was put here by our Creator to do something special. Maybe, like Mangione, it is to make beautiful music. Perhaps our calling is to write, or paint, or dance. Maybe we are here to invent something, start a business, or discover a cure for an illness. Our purpose could be to bring attention to a cause or help end some social problem. Perhaps we're here to be a great parent, teacher, homemaker, or to bake wonderful pies.

Maybe it is some combination of several things. After all, we're complex creative creatures with a wide variety of interests and virtually unlimited capabilities. Whatever your purpose, whatever gets your juices going, you owe it to yourself to pursue it. It's never too soon to begin and it's never too late to start something new.

Grandma Moses, who created some 1,600 works, didn't even begin painting until she was 78 years old and at 92 wrote her autobiography and then continued to paint for about 10 more years.

## So what is it you're too old to do?

Never give up your dreams; never let anyone talk you out of a dream that is important to you. If not for the dreamers this world would be a pretty dull place. Dreamers and visionaries accomplish great feats even though they don't always know exactly how they will do it at the time.

President John F. Kennedy had a dream in 1960 to put a man on the moon by the end of the decade, and on July 21, 1969, Neil Armstrong became the first man to walk on the face of the moon. It's interesting to note that at the time he set the goal, neither he nor NASAknew exactly how they were going to accomplish it.

This is an important point about goal setting. You need not be concerned with how you will accomplish what you want until later in the process. First, you must know your heart's desire.

## What is your purpose?

What really gets your juices going? What matters to you? What comes easily to you? What are you naturally good at? If you're in a transition phase in your life, perhaps nearing retirement to your next adventure or thinking about a career change, these are some of the questions you'll want to be asking yourself.

Notice I said retiring to your next adventure, I did not say retire. As I wrote earlier, I think the idea of retirement is one of the worst things that you can do.

## Action step — What is your adventure?

Later we'll explore some things that you might be interested in, but for now, here is a question that I've used to help me gain clarity about what I really want.

It comes from the noted self-esteem expert Dr. Nathanial Brandon, he asks, "If I were really serious about following my dreams I would _____?"

Write that out on a sheet of paper, or better yet, in your journal and beneath it add five or six lines. Over the next few days think about this and write down everything that comes to mind.

## To dream the impossible dream

What would you do if you knew you would not fail? So many people have a dream, something they have always wanted to do, but do not even attempt it because they are afraid they may not be successful. Others have put their dreams on hold in order to raise a family or have a career. Fortunately, as we age, we reach a point where pursuing our dreams becomes something we can make a priority.

Many people I know have left their big corporate careers having been downsized and tossed out against their will, or took an early retirement, or just decided they're not going to take it anymore and quit.

My wife Georgia left her executive career in telecommunications to follow her own passions. Having a lifelong love of fashion and style and wanting to do something to empower other women and help them feel good about themselves, she began her fashion styling and image consulting business, *The Clothes Doctor*.

> *Never give up on a dream just because of the time it will take to accomplish it. The time will pass anyhow.*
>
> — DR. M. L. KING

Today she gives talks and seminars to companies, associations and women's groups, works with individual clients and has created several home study programs.

She also spends a good portion of her time pursuing her other passion, which is taking care of the furry and feathered creatures who share our home and property with us.

She seems to me to be the happiest while walking around our yard, feeding the animals each morning and when she comes back from a seminar, she's happy and excited about it.

This is a far cry from the days when she would drag herself into the house after a hard day at the office or following a long road trip.

## You're never too old

Often in seminars, someone will say to me, "I'm too old to change" or "I'm too old to follow my dreams." This is pure nonsense. As long as you have a pulse, you can move toward realizing your dreams.

Of course, there are some exceptions. If you're 75 and want to be a professional baseball player, this is not likely to happen, however, there are lots of other dreams you can fulfill regardless of your age.

I've always enjoyed the story about the woman who told author and motivational speaker, Wally Amos, that at 54, if she were to go to law school, in three years when she graduated, she would be 57. Wally asked her how old she would be in three years if she did not go to law school?

I remember a story in the *Philadelphia Inquirer* about a man who had worked in a dry cleaning store for twenty one years without missing a day of work. What made the story unique was that the man was eighty one years old when he was hired! The man, 103 years old when the story was published, was still going strong.

What are some of your dreams? What is it that you would like to have in your life? What would you like to do?

Where would you like to go? Who would you like to meet? What would you like to be known for? What would you like to leave as your legacy?

## Jimmy "the butcher" Smith

A butcher for most of his adult life, Jimmy Smith was content with living a modest, middle class lifestyle. He was a happy man blessed with a loving wife and six children, until at sixty-two years of age he had the rug pulled out from under him. Due to his failing health and being unable to stand all day cutting meat, he was forced to leave the job he had held for most of his life.

While this is surely something that would be a challenge to anyone, in his situation it could have been devastating. Fortunately, for Jimmy, a friend introduced him to the network marketing industry, providing him an opportunity for self-employment and a chance to build a business of his own.

After being in the business for a time, Jimmy Smith found his passion in both the leading edge products and the business opportunity offered by Isagenix International, a company whose vision is to make a positive impact on world health and free people from physical and financial pain, and in the process create the largest health-and-wellness company in the world.

I have personally experienced the Isagenix products and found them to be one of the highest quality nutritional products available as have two of my colleagues John Gray and Jack Canfield.

Jimmy had found his calling. With the the health benefits he realized from taking the Isagenix products and the business opportunity it provided, he was on fire and ready to tell the world about his new business.

When I met Jimmy Smith, a few years ago, he was turning eighty and had the energy and stamina of a man half his age. Not only does he look and feel great, he went on to become the top earner in his company, making himself and his family very wealthy, while building a lasting legacy for his children and grand-children.

Perhaps what best describes Jimmy's energy and passion for what he is doing is the experience that I had while attending an all day event with him. I was leaving the event after being in the hotel for over 12 hours. Riding the elevator down to the lobby with Jimmy's daughter Grace, talking about what a long day it had been, I asked where her dad was. "Oh, he has a few more meetings," she replied. We both laughed at the fact that while we, decades younger, were both ready to call it a day, Jimmy the Butcher was still going strong.

Jimmy Smith is the perfect example of what can happen when a person's passion is ignited by something larger than himself. If you ever have the opportunity to meet Jimmy Smith, by all means, do so. It's a life changing experience.

## Action step — Revisiting your dreams

Take out your journal and find a quiet place where you will not be disturbed. Set aside at least a half hour for this exercise, or do it a little at a time, over a period of several days. You may want to create this as a running list and add to it from time to time.

Georgia and I keep a list we call our "looking forward to" list. This is where we record all the things that we're looking forward to doing. Since we started doing this we have done more, visited more places, seen more movies and plays, been to more restaurants and have had more fun than ever.

If you'd like a real challenge, try this exercise from Jack Canfield and Mark Victor Hansen's book, *The Aladdin Factor.*

Write out 101 wishes on your dreams list. This will challenge you to really think about everything you want to be, do, have and share. It is an exercise that is well worth the effort and one that will reward you with a more exciting and fulfilling life.

The secret in completing this exercise is to really let your mind go. For the time being, don't be concerned with how you will accomplish these things. All you want to do is brainstorm what it is that you would like to be, do, have, and share in your life.

Later on we will extract specific goals from the list and create a plan to help you achieve them, but for now, all you want to do is let your mind run wild. Become like a child again. If you want to travel to some far off place, write it down.

If you want some new possessions, write them down. If you want a new career, write it down. If you want a fabulous relationship, write it down.

If you want to make a difference in your community or in

the world, write it down. Whatever you want, write it on your list. It doesn't have to be realistic.

Just write down everything that comes to mind. Really stretch yourself beyond your comfort zone!

## Your unique gifts and talents

Each of us has unique gifts and talents that we can share with humanity. Unfortunately, many people devote a lot of time thinking about the things that they are not good at instead of focusing on those that they do well.

A person will sit thinking that if they could be like someone else or had a specific talent, then they would be happier. Rather than waste your time wishing you were someone else, build upon the gifts and talents that you already possess.

What are your strengths? Are you great with children? Do you find writing or public speaking something that comes easily to you? Generally, our greatest talents are those things that we truly love to do and are naturally good at. Sometimes we even take them for granted.

When I was a teenager, I played bass guitar in a band. I was a fair guitar player but a very good bass player. My friend Bobby Rivas was a musician. Being around him, I learned the difference between the two, which is why I did not pursue a career in music. Sure, I played professionally for several years and had a lot of fun, but I knew this was not where I would make my mark. I needed to work very hard to learn new songs, since playing music was not something that came easily to me. Bobby, on the other hand, would hear a song once or twice and begin playing it.

One day while we were practicing, his younger brother came home from school with a saxophone. Bobby, who at the time played guitar and piano, began fooling around with the sax. Later that evening he was playing songs on it on stage in the New York City nightclub where we performed. That's a musician!

## Action step — Exploring your gifts and talents

What are your unique gifts? In your journal begin writing some of the things you enjoy and that come naturally. You may well find within this list your ideal future path or something that you would enjoy doing as a business.

For example, if you enjoy meeting and talking with new people and like to help them, working in a sales capacity or becoming a personal coach might be perfect for you. Many people in our society are taking their passion for something and their natural talents and turning them into successful businesses or careers.

If you are reentering the workforce, this exercise can be a valuable first step toward finding work that you will enjoy. I often speak with young people who are graduating from school and are ready for their first job. Unfortunately, they have been conditioned to use their resumes to try to find some job category they can fit into. I say unfortunately because I am of the opinion that there is a better way.

## Creating the life of your dreams

Recently I was speaking with a young woman who was working in a restaurant I frequent. I asked her about her plans since she had finished college. As she began telling me how she was organizing her resume to send out to companies, I could see her expression change from excitement to one of pain at the thought of what she had to do.

Where there should have been joy, enthusiasm, and excitement at the thought of making her first entrance into the business world, there was only pain and apprehension because she was conditioned to believe she had to make herself fit into an available job slot. I was quite saddened seeing this bright, energetic woman starting out this way and found myself coaching her about some better ways she could find work she would enjoy.

My belief is that she can find work she will enjoy, be passionate about, and add significant value to whomever hires her. I urged her to begin to identify her ideal job; one she would look forward to doing each day, rather than simply try to fit into an existing category.

Several years ago, when my business was slow, I sent my resume to a friend who is an Executive Recruiter. He called me right away and apologetically told me that he could not help me. "I'm sorry, Jim," he said "I don't have a pigeon hole you fit into."

After a brief moment of shock, I began to feel really good that I did not fit into any job category. I am a gifted human being and have unique talents I can give to the world. The fact that I did not fit the profile was proof to me that I was on the right track.

> *Whatever you can do or dream you can, begin it. Boldness has genius, power, and magic in it.*
> — GOETHE

Johann Wolfgang von Goethe said "Whatever you can do or dream you can, begin it. Boldness has genius, power, and magic in it."

Alexandra "Alex" Scott only lived 8 years before cancer took her young life. But what a miraculous child. At a very young age, she had the courage and strength to take on her illness, and in spite of being very sick, set out to make a difference. She was only 4 when she decided she wanted to raise funds for research, to help the hospital that was helping her, and to give back to others.

Beginning with just one lemonade stand and the help of her family, *Alex's Lemonade Stands* continue to raise funds to fight cancer. To date, *Alex's Lemonade Stand Foundation* has raised over $25 million for childhood cancer research.

My friend, Cass Forkin, wanted to do something to help

seniors make their dreams come true and began the *Twilight Wish Foundation,* a non-profit foundation that does just that.

One determined woman, with an idea, has been able to grow an organization that, to date, has granted more than 1,135 individual wishes.

You can learn more about both of these groups and how to contact them, in the resource section.

# 3

## CREATE A COMPELLING VISION FOR THE REST OF YOUR LIFE

*"It's better to have no sight, than it is to have no vision"*
HELEN KELLER

If you were living your absolute dream life, what would it look like? What would you be doing? Where and with whom?

It has been said, over and over again, that whatever you can imagine and believe, you can achieve. We'll address beliefs later, but for now let's take a look at getting back in touch with your imagination.

In the last chapter we explored learning to dream again and hopefully you were able to get in touch with many of the things that you would like to do, be, have, and share. Now it's time to learn to use the most powerful resource you have at your disposal. Your imagination.

It is a fact that your subconscious mind, that part of you that is always working, even while you're sleeping, does not know the difference between that which is real and that which is vividly imagined. This is the key to attracting and creating the life you desire.

You may remember back in the 1980's when the Russian Olympic teams were winning all the gold medals. They seemed impossible to beat and were, at least until all the US coaches and trainers learned their "secret." As one story goes, one night the Russian and US trainers were in a cocktail lounge together. The US trainer primed the Russian trainer with vodka and learned their closely guarded secret. Whether the story it true is unimportant however, the lesson is.

What the US Trainer learned was that the Russian athletes were using visualization techniques and mentally rehearsing winning their events. As simple as this may seem now, at the time it was a major breakthrough for the US Olympic teams. Legendary success coach, Dr. Dennis Waitley, was brought in to work with the US teams. Interestingly, his audio program, *The Psychology of Winning*, was the first program of its kind that I was exposed to shortly after I began to rebuild my life and had a profound effect on me. Now, more than twenty years later, I still listen to it. One of the high points of my own career was the day my article on goal setting appeared next to

Dr. Waitley's in a leading success magazine.

When the US teams began using visualization techniques and first, seeing themselves winning gold medals in their imaginations, the actual wins were not far behind.

Legendary golfer Jack Nicklaus said he will not even pick up a club until he has a clear image in his mind as to how the ball will travel and where it will land.

Late in his career Arnold Palmer revealed that he had been using visualization techniques for more than 20 years. He just never felt comfortable enough to talk about it.

When fifteen year old skater Sara Hughes came from behind to win a gold medal, one reporter observed:

"She had visualized herself winning the Olympics since she was a little girl and seemed to sense that her dream was unfolding as she skated. She seemed to seize the moment to fully enjoy giving her performance."

The world famous actor, now Governor of California, Arnold Schwarzenegger, wanted to live in America. He took up weightlifting, since it was at that time, an American sport. Having read about Steve Reeves, a weightlifter who won the Mr. Universe title and went to America to star as *Hercules* in a movie, Schwarzenegger decided this would be his way to accomplish his dreams as well. In his words, he began by "Painting a picture in my mind of myself standing on a pedestal at the Mr. Universe contest and everyone applauding."

That became his vision. He affirmed that he would win the

*Don't Let an Old Person Move Into Your Body*

Mr. Universe title and get into the movies in America. At the time, he was fourteen years old.

With his vision held strongly in his mind, he began training to become a world class weightlifter. When he was twenty years of age, he became the youngest person in history to be crowned Mr. Universe. Three years later, he was cast in his first movie, *Hercules in New York*. The rest, as they say, is history.

Napoleon Hill wrote in *Think and Grow Rich*, in 1937, "the human mind is constantly attracting vibrations which harmonize with that which dominates the mind."

The reason creating vivid images of what we want and visualizing them works, is based on a universal law that has been known for thousands of years. Presently, it's called *The Law of Attraction* and has been written about in several books and explained in the movie, *The Secret*.

Essentially what it means is that any thought, image, or emotion held in our conscious mind, and repeated over and over, will become imprinted on our subconscious, which in turn, will bring it to pass.

This is very powerful and works whether or not we believe in it and with no regard as to whether or not we want what we are focusing upon. *This is important to understand.*

Our subconscious mind does not judge. It brings us whatever we ask for. And we ask with our thoughts, words and feelings. "As a man thinketh in his heart, so is he." Proverbs 23:7. This is an absolute immutable law. As Emerson said, "A man is what he thinks about, all day long."

Unfortunately, the majority of people have not taken the time to learn these ideas, and as a result, live their lives by default. They occupy their minds with a steady stream of negative impressions, delivered each morning and evening in the form of newspapers and TV news.

They then engage in endless discussions with friends and co-workers about "how bad things are" and long for the "good old days." These people unknowingly spend time worrying and thinking about all the bills, never understanding why they can't get ahead. They talk about their illnesses and don't understand why they can't become well.

> *Worrying is using your imagination to create something you do not want.*

It has been said that worrying is using your imagination to create something you do not want.

When I first began studying these ideas over two decades ago, one thing that bothered me and does to this day, is that we do not teach this *mind stuff* to children at a young age.

Imagine how much happier their lives could be if they learned how to harness the incredible powers of their own minds when they were 10 or 12 years old or even younger.

In the classic book *As a Man Thinketh* published in 1902, author James Allen writes "a person's mind may be likened to a garden which may be intelligently cultivated or allowed to run wild, but whether cultivated or neglected, it must and will bring forth."

What have you been planting in the gardens of your mind? Do you spend time talking to anyone who will listen about your latest medical malady, or are you steadily affirming your best health. While we may or may not achieve perfect health, we can, as we'll discuss in a later chapter, begin a program to put ourselves in the best health possible for us.

Do you complain about the economy and what *they* should be doing with your money? Or have you taken responsibility for your own financial security? Throughout history, there have been people who have remained affluent, regardless of the economy or government.

The key to having the kind of life you want, and are entitled to, is to first and foremost, create a vivid image of it in your mind.

Later in this chapter, I will ask you to complete a vision activity detailing how you would like each key area of your life to be. Please take the time to do this as completely as possible. This one relatively simple act will do more to help you create a fantastic future then anything else you can do.

Everything begins with a vision. If you're planning on building your dream home, you would not just start digging a hole in the ground. You would first, with an architect, develop an exact representation of what the house will look like when it is completed. You would include every detail in your drawing. Nothing would be left out. Of course, you'll make changes along the way; your vision is not carved in stone.

The challenge for most of us is maintaining balance in our lives. Generally, people excel in one area of life, like finances or fitness, at the expense of others. To live a truly happy and fulfilling life requires balance between several areas. Whenever I complete a vision or goal setting exercises, I include all the key areas of my life.

## Example — my vision

My life is awesome! My health is fantastic. I beam with energy and look and feel fit, trim and healthy. I honor and love my body and take great care of it. I always have boundless energy. I jump out of bed early each day, eager to greet the new day. I feel so vibrant and healthy.

I am jazzed about my work. My books fly off the shelves reaching and helping millions of people throughout the world. This feels great.

My work is having a massive positive effect on the lives of people everywhere, and I am honored and thrilled to be doing this. I feel so successful and appreciated. My life is magnificent and I love every minute of it.

## Action step — Your compelling vision

What about you? If you were living your ideal life, what would it look like? Where would you be living, what would you be doing with your time? Who would you be sharing your life with? Would you travel? Where? How much money would you have?

For the sake of this exercise, pick a timeframe between one and three years. You can always come back to this section and do another one for a longer period of time.

One of the reasons Japanese businesses have been so successful beginning from virtually nothing after World War II to becoming a world power today, is because Japanese companies create long-term visions and goals. It is not unusual for a Japanese company to be working from a 50 year vision.

> *If you don't know where you're going, any road will take you there.*
> — CHESHIRE CAT

Of course, they do not know precisely what the world will look like in 50 years, but by having a general vision of what they want the company to be, they have a beacon to guide their actions. Like the Cheshire cat said to Alice in Alice in Wonderland, "If you don't know where you're going, any road will take you there."

In your vision, be sure to include something from each of the following categories:

## Spirituality and Religion

In three years what is your relationship to your Creator? Do you spend time each day in prayer and meditation? Are you involved with your church, synagogue or mosque? Are you living a spiritual life? How is this being reflected in your day to day life? What is your connection to your community?

## Self-development

What have you done to enrich your mind? Have you added to your education? Did you obtain a degree or learn a new skill? Have you studied a new language? What are you doing regularly to expand your mind? How many books have you read? How many audio programs have you listened to? Have you attended seminars or taken a class in something? Do you make a habit of reading uplifting, inspirational material each day? Doing this for just ten or fifteen minutes a day will help you keep a positive attitude and will contribute more to your happiness than any other action you can take.

## Health and Fitness

How is your health? Are you becoming more fit? What are you doing to nurture yourself regularly? Do you exercise? What about sports and leisure activities? Have you taken up a sport, such as golf or tennis? Are you steadily improving your eating habits to become healthier? Do you have regular medical checkups? Are you taking extraordinary care of your body? Do you have massages, facials or other types of body work? Do you take time for yourself and actively work to reduce stress? Have you studied yoga, tai-chi, Qi-gong, or something to help you relax and increase your physical fitness? Are you taking vitamin supplements?

## Family and Relationships

What about your relationships? Do you have a great relationship with your spouse and loved ones? What about friends? Have you developed meaningful relationships with people who support you and have your best interests in mind? Are you supportive and nurturing to your friends as well? Have you found ways to maintain romance in your significant relationship?

## Career and Business

In your three year vision, where have you gone in your career or business? What is your work day like? What are the feelings you experience in your chosen work? How great is it? Have you begun your own business? How has it grown? What are you doing each day? Where are you contributing to society? Remember the idea of having a big vision, one that will excite you just thinking about living it.

## Social and Material

What are you doing socially? Have you seen a number of plays, concerts or movies? Where are you vacationing? Have you taken your family to a great restaurant? What are you doing? What do you own? Do you have a new luxury auto-mobile? A boat? A plane? A summer house at the beach? Have you added an incredible media center to your home? A new computer? New furniture? A great wardrobe? Do you have a special piece of jewelry or watch that you've always wanted? What have you been able to buy for your family?

## Money and Investments

How much money are you earning? What have you invested in? How much are you saving each month? What are you using your money for? Are you tithing regularly to your place of worship or favorite charity?

> *If you want a big life, you need big dreams.*
>
> — N. V. PEALE

These are just some examples of the kinds of questions that you can ask yourself as you create your personal vision. Make it big, bright, powerful, and exciting. As the late Norman Vincent Peale, considered to be one the pioneers of the modern self-help movement, said, "If you want a big life, you need big dreams."

Great! You now have an inspiring, motivating, rich vision of how you want your life to be in three years. I strongly suggest that you take the time to read it each day. This act alone will begin to draw it toward you and greatly increase your chance of it becoming a reality. Reading your vision with excitement and passion will also help you begin each day with your personal energy in alignment with what you most want, thereby attracting it to you. You may even want to record this and play it back for yourself. Remember the universe works on the principal of like attracts like. The more you put yourself in the energetic state of that which you want, and experience the feelings of having it, the faster you will attract it to you.

Spend some time each day, in your imagination, experiencing the feelings of already living your dream life. Create your own "mind movie" in which you are living this imagined life.

If it's a vacation home you want, see yourself walking through it and looking out at the views. If it's better health you desire, see yourself looking the way you want to look. Make it real. Remember, your subconscious mind does not know the difference between what is real and that which is vividly imagined.

## Breaking it down

Now that you have a clear idea of where you want to be and what you want your life to become, it is time to extract some specific measurable goals you can achieve in the next twelve months. We will then break these down even further, and finally, develop an action plan to keep you on track.

Looking back over each area of your vision, choose one or two specific goals that you can accomplish in a year's time;

goals that will move you toward fulfilling your vision.

For example, if in your vision you are living a carefree life, with plenty of money, doing work you love, a one-year goal that would lead you towards your vision might be to start your own business and begin earning a specific amount of money from it.

Write your goal in the present tense as though it has already happened and state it in the positive. Your subconscious mind does not understand time. If you write, "I *will* be healthy and fit," it will remain out of your reach. It also does not recognize the reverse of an idea. If I say, "Don't think of a green elephant," what happens?

If you say, "I want to lose 20 pounds," it's not as effective as saying, "I am so happy that I weigh 120 pounds and feel great." Always write goals and affirmations in the present tense and phrase them in a positive manner.

Be sure to make it exciting and colorful, too. Your one year business goal might read like this: *"I am so happy and grateful now that I have my own business, making a difference and earning an additional twenty five thousand dollars a year from it."*

If, in your vision you have a great, loving, supportive, respectful, special relationship with another person, your goal might read like this: *"I am so happy and grateful now that I am in a warm, loving, passionate relationship with the perfect life partner."* Another might be, *"I am so happy and grateful that I am blessed with supportive and loving friends who I enjoy spending time with."*

I like to start an affirmation with the phrase, "I am so happy and grateful" because that, in and of itself, sets up a positive, attraction energy and reaffirms my being happy and grateful. Gratitude is one of the highest vibrational states we can achieve.

Affirmations are powerful and they are one of the best ways to implant your desires into your subconscious mind. In *Think and Grow Rich*, Napoleon Hill devoted an entire chapter to the power of "auto suggestion," also known as "self suggestion," as a way to change any belief or behavior.

I personally became a non-smoker after about 30 years of being addicted to cigarettes using an affirmation that I learned from Louise Hay.

The specific phrase that I used, for anyone wanting to change unproductive behavior, is "I now release the need for cigarettes." Notice that I did not say, "give up." We humans do not usually "give up" anything without a fight. Releasing the need is quite different from giving up or quitting.

Remember your words have power. I would write my affirmation sometimes 25 or 50 times a day, recite them, even sing them while driving in the car.

The more you repeat an affirmation, the faster it works, however you must do so with feeling and see yourself as having already accomplished your goal. Our emotions and feelings are what attracts to us, so simply reciting an affirmation without emotion and belief will probably not work.

Remember, "Whatever you ask for in prayer, believe that you will receive it and it is yours." Mark 11:24-25 (NIV)

## Action step — Goal setting

In your journal complete this activity. Choose one or two goals from each of the areas in your vision that you could accomplish in one year. Choose goals that are in alignment with the vision you completed earlier.

By the way, if you already have your own business, you may want to complete a vision and goal session for it, and if you have employees or a team, have each of them do the same. Companies using these principals have produced quantum leaps in their revenue. As I said before, you can use these techniques for any area of your life.

Create one or two simple affirmations that support your new vision and goals and use them daily.

The alternative is leaving your life to chance. The fact that you're reading this book tells me that you are not one of those people willing to settle and live, as Henry David Thoreau said, "in quiet desperation." You have within you the power to change your life and within this book are the tools and techniques to help you do it.

# 4

## WHATSOEVER YOU BELIEVE

B eliefs are one of my favorite subjects. If there is one thing that will keep you from having everything you want in your life, it is what you believe about yourself, your abilities, and the world in which you live.

Everything that you do in your life and everything that you have accomplished, will ever accomplish, or even attempt to accomplish, is directly governed by your beliefs.

### Where do beliefs come from?

Abelief, quite simply, is something that you have told yourself over and over throughout your life. Beliefs start at a young age. If we try something for the first time and we fail, we label ourselves a failure. For example, if at the age of 10 or 12, I attempted to play basketball, but because of my age and size was not very good at it, I may have created a belief in my own mind that I cannot play basketball. This was probably not true, since beliefs rarely are.

A more common example is the person who once tried their own business but was not successful. They created a belief that they are not meant to be in business, and therefore, never tried it again. This is really sad when you consider that almost every successful business person has experienced many "failures." The difference is in the way they viewed the experience and the beliefs that they created from them. One person may see a business "failure" as a sign they cannot be a successful business owner, while the other will only view it as a temporary set-back and turn it into a learning experience.

> *Whether you believe*
> *you can or you*
> *believe you can't,*
> *you're right.*
> — HENRY FORD

The same holds true for weight loss. A person may have gone on a diet or weight loss program, and for whatever reason, did not produce the results they had hoped for. Worse yet, they may have lost a certain amount of weight only to gain it back, and more, a short time later.

They labeled themselves a failure and accepted, *as fact*, that they cannot lose weight. They may even make excuses like, "I have big bones." Their inability to lose weight permanently is nothing more than a belief, and likely, the result of having chosen the wrong program or having followed a fad diet.

Becoming physically fit, like most things, requires you to follow a proven program and/or model the behavior of someone who has successfully done it.

## Other people's beliefs

Perhaps the most limiting and destructive beliefs are those we are given by other people and society in general. There is something called a "global belief," which is what happens when a whole section of society agrees that something is true.

Many of the long held global beliefs that were later proven to be false include, "Man was not meant to fly" and "the world is flat."

In the case of Roger Bannister, the first human being to break the four minute mile, it was believed that, "Man cannot run a mile in under four minutes." That particular belief survived for thousands of years before Mr. Bannister came along and shattered it. Now, it's not unusual for college athletes to run a sub-four minute mile.

Many times a child is told "You can't do that, you're too small," and believing the adult, the child carries this belief with them throughout their lives. They begin to apply it to everything that is a challenge. They think, "I can't do that, I'm too small," and continue to see themselves as being too small in the world.

## Why the elephants don't run

A number of years ago, I had the rather unique experience of visiting backstage in Madison Square Garden, in New York, during the Ringling Brothers Barnum & Bailey Circus. To say the least, it was a fascinating experience. I was able to walk around looking at the lions, tigers, giraffes and all the other circus animals. As I was passing the elephants, I suddenly stopped, confused by the fact that these huge creatures were being held by only a small rope tied to their front leg. No chains, no cages. It was obvious that the elephants could, at any time, break away from their bonds but for some reason, they did not. I saw a trainer nearby and asked why these beautiful, magnificent animals just stood there and made no attempt to get away.

"Well," he said, "when they are very young and much smaller we use the same size rope to tie them, and at that age, it's enough to hold them. As they grow up, they are conditioned to stand there. They believe the rope can still hold them, so they never try to break free."

I was amazed. These animals could at any time break free from their bonds, *but* because they believed they couldn't, they were stuck right where they were. I am not, by the way, endorsing this horrible treatment of animals. On the contrary. Only when we treat all living things as having value, will we truly value ourselves.

## What are your ropes?

Like the elephants, how many of *you* go through life hanging onto a belief that you cannot do something, simply because you failed at it once before? How many of *you* are being held back by old, outdated beliefs that no longer serve you? How many of *you* have avoided trying something new because of a limiting belief? Worse, how many of you are being held back by *someone else's* limiting beliefs?

## How your beliefs determine your results

Let's take a closer look at exactly how our beliefs determine results. Most people would agree that we have unlimited potential. Why then do we not see this in the results that we produce?

This is where beliefs come into play. The result you produce is determined by the actions you take. The problem is, most of us have a limiting belief in our ability to accomplish a particular task. We only tap into a small portion of our potential, take limited action and produce a poor result.

An example of this principal is the dieter who tries eating healthier for a few days but then gives up, because they believe they cannot successfully lose weight.

Another example is the home business person who makes a few calls before deciding that this product is not right for them and moves on to join yet another company.

In both cases, it was the person's limiting belief in their

own ability that caused them to take such little action in the first place.

Fortunately, the opposite is also true. If you develop a belief you can do whatever you set your mind to, you will tap into more of your limitless potential, take massive amounts of action, and produce even greater results.

My favorite example of this principal is the story of one of my mentors and favorite people, Jack Canfield, the co-author of the *Chicken Soup for the Soul* series of books. Jack and his co-author Mark Victor Hansen, were turned down more than 140 times when they were first trying to get their book published.

Because of their strong belief in themselves and their book they persevered, talking to publisher after publisher, until finally, at the *American Booksellers Association* conference, a relatively unknown publisher decided to take a chance and publish the book.

*Chicken Soup for the Soul* has gone on to break all sales records for non-fiction books and has expanded into numerous spin off editions and related products.

All of this was possible because of the strongly held belief that Jack and Mark had about their ability to succeed and a deeply held belief in the value of their wonderful book.

It was their belief that made them unstoppable and motivated them to continue to take massive action and not give up. When asked what they would have done, had their publisher not agreed to publish the book, they said they would have kept on asking.

We will consistently perform in accordance with what we believe about ourselves, our capabilities, and about the world we live in. This is why it is so important, so crucial, to create beliefs that will empower us, and help us become the people that we know we are capable of becoming.

## The courage to change

It's not always easy to change. Often it means doing new things and letting go of beliefs you may have held for most of your life. If you really want to live the life you deserve, it's essential to let go of those beliefs that are not supporting you. We've all said at one time or another, "That's just the way I am." This is like the severely overweight person who says, "I have big bones." Nonsense! Anyone can change their beliefs about themselves, and in the next few pages we will explore ways to do just that.

## Removing the illusion

Any belief that you have about yourself is the result of a combination of several things. It is something that you have told yourself over and over again or others have told you over and over again until you believe it to be true. The driving force behind our beliefs, and perhaps the strongest determinate, are the references that we have created to support a given belief.

As I said before, if a person has gone on a diet and not lost more than a few pounds, very often they will create a belief that they are "not able to lose weight." Their failed attempt becomes the reference that supports their belief. They say things like, "See, I tried but I just can't do it."

I once spoke with a woman who had written a wonderful children's book and when I asked her about having it published she told me she had tried but no publisher wanted to take it on. This, of course, was merely a belief.

I questioned her further about having submitted the book to children's book publishers and she replied that she had done so. I asked, "How many?" She replied, "Three." She had sent her book to a mere three publishers, and when they declined, she created a belief that no one wanted to publish her book and gave up.

In contrast, as I said before, the authors of *Chicken Soup for the Soul* presented their manuscript to more than 140 publishers before finding one that agreed to publish it.

Thomas Edison tried more than 10,000 times to invent the electric light, before he finally succeeded. When asked what he would have done had he not found the answer, he replied, "I would have kept on looking."

One way to begin to shift your limiting beliefs is to question the references that are supporting them and replace them with new ones that will empower you to create what you want. References are like the legs on a stool; they support the belief. If you begin to break down the references, you weaken the belief the same way that you would weaken the stool if you began to break the legs.

In the case of the woman with the children's book, all she had to do was realize that although three publishers turned her down, there are more than 50,000 publishers in the United States alone. It would have been obvious that believing "no one wants to publish my book" was pure nonsense. The truth of the matter was that she was not committed enough to keep going. She could have created a belief that, "There are plenty of publishers left. I'm sure one will want my book."

She could have followed the example of my friends, Laura Duksta and Karen Keesler, authors of *I Love You More*. They chose to self-publish their wonderful children's book, and after having achieved a level of success, were able to get the attention of a big publisher. When we last spoke, their book had reached number seven on the *New York Times Bestseller List*, a significant accomplishment for any author.

Let's begin now to shift some of your limiting beliefs.

## Moving through the gap

There is always a gap between your present circumstance and the life you want to be living. It's human nature to want to experience more in your life, while still being appreciative of what you have.

Who among us does not want more love, vibrant health, a

more fulfilling relationship with our loved ones, more challenging work, more creativity, and yes, more money? If it were not for people wanting more material possessions, most of the great companies in the world would not exist and much of the world's population would not have jobs.

If people like Bill Gates (Microsoft), Akio Morita (Sony), Sakichi Toyota (Toyota), Coco Chanel, (Chanel), or Mary Kay Ash, (Mary Kay) were satisfied with creating just enough for themselves, the thousands of people who work for their companies would be unemployed.

The people who believe it is somehow wrong or greedy to want more, simply do not understand the world in which we live.

Yes, there are greedy people, however, when I refer to wanting more, I'm referring to people like you and I who want to create more not only to help ourselves and our loved ones, but hopefully, to have a positive impact on society as well. It is possible for the entire population of the world to live in abundance. The only limits in our world are those imposed by ourselves through what we choose to believe.

God's universe knows no lack. If you doubt this, go out and count the number of seeds in a tomato and realize that each is capable of producing an entire plant which will bring many, many more tomatoes, and so on. Or try to count the blades of grass in a lawn or the trees in a forest. The only lack in our world is a result of our own thinking.

The only difference between where you are right now and

having what you want is a belief. For example, I believe I drive a Lexus automobile. I believe it because it is in my garage. This was not always the case. There was a time, years ago, when I was without a car and walked or took the bus everywhere. Then there was a time, after that, when I drove a beat up old car that would break down on a regular basis.

What it took for me to attract the Lexus into my life was to begin to believe I deserve to have it and then to do the work that would make it possible for me to afford it. I had, as I wrote earlier, to begin to *see* myself living at this level.

## Overcoming resistance

Where a lot of people have problems with setting and achieving goals is that the gap between where they are and where they want to be is so huge their mind cannot believe it is possible to have what they want. Sure, writing goals and repeating affirmations about what you want will eventually bring it to you, but more often than not, people give up before they reach their goals because their internal belief is so strong that it overrides their desire.

So how do we get past this? I use a technique called a "bridge belief." It's really quite simple. Consider your current reality as a starting point. For example, "I can't make enough money," is a belief shared by many people.

Let's suppose your goal is "financial independence." In order to have financial independence you would need to believe that you have lots of money.

Can you see the huge gap between these two realities? On one side of the gap, "I can't make enough money," and on the other side of the gap, "I have lots of money." Trying to shift from a belief of "I have no money" to a belief of "I have lots of money," is like trying to jump the Grand Canyon on a motorcycle. This is something that was attempted by a dare devil named Evel Knievel, who was seriously injured when he tried to do it.

A more effective method of achieving what you want is to gradually move toward it by shifting your beliefs a little at a time. For example, a new belief you could affirm, which your subconscious would accept, might be "I am in the process of increasing my income." This particular phrase is from one of the best books I've read about the law of attraction, appropriately titled, *Law of Attraction,* by Michael Losier.

While this is not the desired end result of "I have lots of money," it is further along than the original, low energy belief and will begin to move you in the direction of your dreams.

What you're essentially doing is raising your *energetic vibration.* As your present conditions begin to shift to a better place, you can create another bridge belief that is even closer to your desired outcome until, one day, your desire and your reality are the same and you have whatever it is you want. By using the bridge belief, you will begin feeling better and be moving toward what you want.

## Your bridge belief

Think about one thing that you really, really want to change. Perhaps it's your weight. What is your current situation? Is it, "I'm overweight and out of shape"? What is your desired reality? Is it, "I look and feel great and I am healthy and fit"? This is obviously a long way from where you are now.

You could work with a new affirmation such as, "I am in the process of becoming healthier. I am exercising, eating smarter, and becoming healthier each day."

While this may not be all the way to your goal, it will make you feel better than your current belief. The better you begin to feel about yourself, the more motivated you will be to achieve your goal.

## Action step — Bridge beliefs

What is your number one challenge?

What is your current belief? (I can't ever lose weight)

What is your desired reality ?(I am fit and healthy)

Create your bridge belief (I am in the process of achieving my best health.)

By affirming your new bridge belief, which you believe because it is true, you'll produce feelings that are higher than the low energy feeling you have now. These new feelings will help you move toward your desired goals. As you progress, you will change your bridge belief to match your new, improved reality until, one day, it will match what you want and you will have it.

## Beware of the "if then" trap

Do you find yourself saying things like "If only I had such and such, then I would be happy"? Do you have a dream that is really burning inside you but think you'll never achieve it because of some insurmountable obstacle? Did you create the obstacle in your mind or did someone else put it there?

In my coaching practice I consistently notice these walls standing between people and their dreams. Interestingly enough, the wall is usually in the person's own mind and not really the obstacle that they think it is.

Very often it's not even theirs but was put there by some well intentioned friend or family member. Once we remove the wall, the person is on their way to living their dreams.

## Taking down the walls

One way that you can begin to remove your walls or blocks is to use a powerful question. Powerful questions are something used by coaches to help people move through whatever is blocking them.

For example, you could ask yourself something like, "How could I accomplish what I want with the resources I presently have?" This simple, yet powerful question, literally changed my life.

Years ago, I had an idea for a video program. The problem was I did not have the necessary resources to produce a video. Broadcast quality video production can be quite expensive. I spent several years with my idea sitting dormant, deluding myself that "someday I'll be able to produce it." One day, which happened to be my birthday, I was listening to a personal development audio when the author suggested that I use the above question to shift my thinking and take down the wall I had built.

When I applied the question "What resources do I presently have?" to my idea of producing a video, I realized that while I may not have been in a position to produce the video, I did have the resources necessary to write and produce a book. That day I began writing my first book. My life has never been the same since.

> *How could I accom - plish what I want with the resources I presently have?*

Interestingly enough, that book was never published, however, writing it led me to a totally new career and a clear sense of my purpose. I have written and published several books, which have been translated into other languages, and are sold throughout the world. All this is the result of asking a different, more empowering, question.

So often we erect these huge walls that limit our progress and keep us from our dreams. By using a different question you can uncover alternative methods to accomplish your goal. By using a different question you can become unstuck and move toward what you desire.

A friend and client of mine had a dream to build a healing and counseling center. Looking at her business plan, I noticed a huge wall standing in her way. The plan called for almost a million dollars in start-up capital. When I asked her why she needed so much money she replied, "To buy the building." I could easily see this was not essential. I asked her if and how she could begin right now with what she had, without the building. I saw a sparkle in her eyes as she realized that it was possible to begin her business right then and there, with the resources she had. Her original business plan is still intact, however, she is now moving in the direction of her dream.

The building was not the business or the dream. The dream was to help people, and once we uncovered that, the building became unnecessary. It was merely a wall that stood between her and her passion. With the wall removed she is free to pursue a life long dream of helping people heal. I am certain that one day she will have her building, but in the meantime, she is doing what she loves.

## Action step — Take down the walls

If you want to move toward creating the life of your dreams, complete the following exercise:

What walls have you or someone else erected?

How else might you accomplish your objective using the resources you already have?

How could you begin right now?

Who can help?

What immediate action could you take to move in the direction of your desire?

# 5

## ATTITUDE IS EVERYTHING

In order for you to live a happy and productive life it is necessary for you to take control of your emotions, rather than letting them control you. Whatever emotion you're experiencing is the result of thinking a particular thought. The thought will trigger an internal dialog that will cause the emotional state. The states that I'm referring to here and the ones that you will want to take control of are those undesirable states like rage, anger, overwhelm, fear, helplessness, and other emotional states that you may experience regularly that are blocking your progress.

### Motion equals emotion

The fastest way I know to change an unwanted emotional state is to start moving. That's right, move! The next time you're feeling down or depressed, get up and go for a walk. Of course, I'm not referring to clinical depression. If you suffer from constant depression, please seek professional help. I'm talking about those moods we all experience from time to time. By changing your physiology, you will change your emotional state. This is one reason why people usually feel happier after rigorous exercise. Just taking a brisk walk, run or swim will help you to feel better and increase your mental capacity and creativity. Physical movement will always have a positive affect on your emotional state.

## Changing your state with music

Music is a powerful emotional trigger that you can use to recreate a desirable emotional or mental state. There are times when I am going to speak to a group and I'm not feeling at my peak energy level. The group listening to me, however, deserves me at my very best, so I have developed several rituals to help raise my energy. One of the most powerful ones is music. I keep some very specific music on my iPod™ to play while I am on my way there. One song, in particular, that instantly puts me in a peak state, is Billy Joel's, *We Didn't Start the Fire.*

This song was played at the Anthony Robbins *Fear Into Power—the Fire Walk Experience* seminar that I participated in many years ago. It was where I confronted my fears by walking barefoot over a bed of hot coals. Whenever I hear that song I immediately connect with the intense energy and peak emotion that I experienced that night as I was preparing to walk over the coals. It was a life altering experience to say the least. Playing that song immediately changes my energy level regardless of how I may be feeling at the time. Music creates powerful "anchors" that can take us back to almost any point in time. How many times have you heard a song from your youth and immediately went back in time, remembering the details of the event, even though it may be decades later?

If you were to come home from work totally exhausted and wanted to do nothing more than sit and watch TV and I walked in and handed you $50,000 to go out and buy whatever you wanted, provided you went out right away, do you think you could muster the energy to do it? Of course you could. You would immediately forget that you were tired and jump up ready to go.

Rarely are we actually as tired as we think. More often than not, our feeling tired is a mental drain not a physical state and can be quickly altered by changing our emotional focus.

If you want to easily recreate a pleasant emotional state, keep some music around that has special meaning to you and will make you feel good. The song *I Got You* (I Feel Good) by James Brown, is one that will have a positive effect on almost everyone. Other songs that tend to have a positive effect are *Celebration*, by Kool and the Gang, from the late 1970's and *Soak Up the Sun* by Sheryl Crow.

Select some music, from your collection, that will trigger happy thoughts for you and keep it nearby, or better yet, begin your day by listening to it.

## Change your life

My friend Vinny Roazzi, in his book *The Spirituality of Success* wrote, "If you want to change your life, you have to change your life." What this means is that if you want to make changes and experience your life at a different level, *you* must be willing to change.

> *If you want to change your life, you have to change your life.*
>
> — VINNY ROAZZI

Once you begin to change your beliefs about what is possible for your life, you must be willing to do what it takes. This usually requires you to change some of your habits and activities. When my life began to turn around, after hitting my lowest point, it became clear to me that I would have to make significant changes if I was to have the kind of life I wanted.

The path I was on was going nowhere but down, and if I did not change, I would probably die, or worse—continue to live in the misery that my life had become. I was in so much spiritual, mental, physical and emotional pain that I would have done anything to change my life.

I changed my habits. I changed where I lived and my work.

I even changed the kind of music I listened to. I went from "party animal" to becoming a quiet, reflective person. I traded late nights and crazy times for early mornings and solitude.

I asked God to come back into my life and reconnected with my spirituality. Having been a night owl, I changed my sleeping habits and learned to like getting up early in the morning, about the same time I used to come in from a night on the town. I'm not suggesting that everyone do this or that there is anything wrong with partying, but this is what I had to do since the life I was leading was literally killing me.

All too often I hear people talking about how they want their lives to change. Some want a better relationship, to lose weight, start a business, or earn more money. However, they continue doing the same things they have always done. Nothing changes. It can't be both ways. One definition of insanity, is doing the same thing and expecting a different result.

If you want to change your life, you must change your life. If you want to weigh less and be healthier, it is necessary to embark on a regular exercise program and make healthier food choices.

If what you want is financial independence and security, you will need to change your relationship with money. You may need to learn more about finances and investments, change your spending habits, or some combination of both. You may want to begin your own part or full-time business. We'll discuss finance in greater detail later in this book, but for now, just realize that anything that you want that you do not already have will require some form of change.

The person who wants a better relationship with their spouse or children might need to change the way they relate to and communicate with them. The parent who wants a better relationship with their child, but is busy working, may want to reevaluate their priorities and make some changes in their schedule to allow more time for their children.

Time with family is one of the main reasons so many people are starting their own businesses and working from home. Many parents are finding that working from home gives them the extra time to devote to their children's upbringing and makes it easier to juggle a family and career.

What changes will you make? Do you spend your spare time surfing the Internet or watching television, when what you really want is financial freedom? Doing what you're presently doing will not get you there. Perhaps trading a night of television to take a class to learn a new skill will move you closer to your dream life.

If you want to learn more about finance, business or investments, there are plenty of evening programs you can enroll in that will teach you what you need to know. You can even find programs that you can take right on the Internet.

If you want to have better health, you could trade some of your "couch potato" time and join a health club or enroll in a yoga or Tai Chi class.

## Your self image

It is impossible for a person to act or behave in a manner that is inconsistent with how he or she sees themselves. It is equally impossible for you to be in a resourceful state, demonstrating your best and highest capabilities, if you are consistently putting yourself down, or worse yet, allowing other people to belittle you.

What you tell yourself over and over is one of the major contributors to whatever level of success you achieve in any area of your life. What you listen to from other people is another key influencer of your behavior. Both of these, self-talk and talk from others, molds us and drives our behavior in any given situation.

## Your words have power

First, let's examine our self-talk more closely. Throughout the day, during every waking hour, we are carrying on a running dialogue with ourselves. We are constantly thinking, or more accurately, talking to ourselves in every waking moment.

Hundreds of words per minute pass through our conscious minds as we go about our day. Unfortunately, for one reason or another, most people's self-talk is negative. This is probably due to the number of negative messages we heard as we were growing up and continue to hear today.

These came from other, perhaps well intentioned, people or

individuals who were themselves living in a negative reality. Much of it is from a steady stream of negativity bombarding us from television, radio, newspapers and magazines.

Situation comedies, for the most part, belittle people in the name of humor and many game and reality shows place people in embarrassing situations further undermining their self-image.

The other day I was sitting outside a local restaurant writing while enjoying a quiet lunch. It was a beautiful spring day and the restaurant provided me with a view of the Delaware River, near where I live. Access to scenes like this is one of the many reasons I feel so blessed to be living the life that I am living and further proof, to me, of the power of creating a compelling vision for your life.

Where we live is the result of my wife and I becoming clear as to exactly what we wanted in our life, setting specific goals, visualizing our dream life as already complete, and taking regular action. I don't just write about these principles, I live them daily and have for over two decades. And I've seen magnificent changes in my life as a result. Remember, we ask, God answers.

As I was sitting there totally enjoying the scenery, two women walked passed me on their way out of the restaurant, having finished their lunch. The women looked to be in their late 40's or early 50's although I avoid *ever* guessing women's ages for obvious reasons.

As they passed, I overheard one of the women say, "When I

was young . . ." Those words hit me like a lighting bolt, especially since I was working on this book at the time.

What a disempowering choice of words. Your words have power, so choose them carefully. While you and I know that she meant no harm by her choice of that particular phrase, her mind took it in. What do you suppose the message to her subconscious mind was? Obviously, I'm not young any longer. I must be old!

A phrase that would have conveyed the same message but would have been more empowering would have been to say, "When I was younger . . ."

Without even realizing it, you're programming your mind with disempowering, less than ideal, messages. Keep in mind that your subconscious believes everything that you tell it.

Think about the phrases that you use regularly to describe yourself or how you feel and make sure that they are sending a positive message to your subconscious mind. Avoid any phrase that is negative or dis-empowering.

As a matter of fact, by amplifying positive words like saying "great or terrific" instead of just "good or fine," and minimizing negative ones, you can actually improve the way you feel.

Years ago, when I had the pleasure of meeting and briefly speaking with success legend, Zig Ziglar, I remember his reply to my question, "How are you?" Zig's answer, "Better than great."

## What are you saying to yourself?

Stop beating yourself up. When you make a mistake how do you respond? What do you say to yourself when you have trouble figuring out a computer program, for example? I have heard people tell themselves how stupid they are and how they never do anything right, simply because they had trouble with a new software program. This is not only absurd and not true, it is quite damaging to your self-esteem.

What are you telling yourself? When you make a mistake do you view it as just that, a mistake? Do you learn from it and make a point not to repeat it? Or do you start belittling yourself with a stream of negative self-talk? Do you recognize, as one of Billy Joel's song titles suggests, *You're Only Human,* and lighten up on yourself?

One of the reasons I have been able to learn new things easily is because growing up, my mother would tell me how smart I was. Being a young child, I believed this and began to behave in a manner consistent with her opinion. While in my teenage years I was a poor student and didn't like school, feeling it was too structured. I've always found it easy to learn new things. When I reached an age where I saw the value of learning, I did so with ease. In television electronics school in the military, I finished second in my class.

To this day, I have a belief that learning is fun and easy and reinforce that belief with my self-talk. This serves me well especially in our rapidly changing technological world. I take to new ideas and technology like a fish takes to water.

As we discussed earlier, we behave and perform in a manner that is consistent with what we believe about ourselves. Our beliefs are molded by what we tell ourselves over and over again. When you do something well, recognize it and reinforce the positive behavior with positive self-talk. When you make a mistake, see that it is just that, a mistake, realizing you are only human, tell yourself you'll do better next time. Use the power of your self-talk to help develop the habits and characteristics you want to create.

For example, when I am running on the treadmill at my health club, I repeat an affirmation I learned from Dr. Deepak Chopra "Every day in every way I am increasing my mental and physical capacity." I consistently reinforce my exercise with positive self-talk, noticing my progress, and telling myself how great I feel.

> *Every day in every way I am increasing my mental and physical capacity.*
>
> — DEEPAK CHOPRA

Author and speaker Brian Tracy suggests that people in sales repeat the phrase, "I'm a great sales person" over and over for a few minutes prior to making a sales call. This conditions your mind for success and helps support a healthy self-image.

I frequently speak to groups who are at the lower end of the socio-economic scale and are struggling to improve their lives. I do this, because, having been in that situation, I am able to connect with these people. When they realize I have been at the bottom too and have changed my life, they see it is possible for them to do the same thing. I am able to get my message across, and I personally get a lot of satisfaction seeing a person believe they can change and begin seeing themselves differently.

What I've noticed among these groups of people is that their self-talk, along with their self-image, tends to be quite negative. They are quick to put themselves down and are very hard on themselves for even the slightest thing. Much of this is the result of the environment from which they came.

I'll never forget one woman who, during a group workshop, asked me what I would do if everyone around me was always putting me down and belittling me. I replied simply, "I'd get away from them." These are the people my friend, Jack Canfield, refers to as "toxic people." They are poisonous to your well-being.

These are the people in your life, sometimes quite close to you, who keep trying to make you feel less than you are. Often, they believe that this is the way to motivate people. It's not! Perhaps they just want to make sure that you don't succeed and leave them behind.

Whatever their reasons, it is important for you to either get away from them, or at the very least, learn to ignore what they tell you. If someone close to you is telling you that you are stupid and will never get ahead, you can be saying to yourself, "You're wrong, I'm already getting ahead and becoming more successful each day," or something like that. Often we hear these negative messages at a very young age and carry them with us throughout our lives, replaying them over and over again.

I can still hear my grandfather's voice, from when I was an adolescent, telling me I was a lazy bum, just like my father and I would never amount to anything. I believe he loved me and that this was his way of getting me to change what were becoming some very poor habits and life choices. However, it did not work. All this did was undermine my already fragile self-esteem and make me feel worthless. I carried that message and replayed it in my own head for many years before I learned a better way.

We don't even realize the devastating impact such harsh words and criticism can have on a young person's mind. Children believe what they are told by the adults in their lives. One of the reasons we have such problems in our society with teenage alcohol and drug abuse is a lack of self-esteem. I know one thing with absolute certainty.

If you have a healthy self-image, you do not need to abuse drugs or alcohol, commit crimes, or harm yourself or anyone else. One of the solutions to the problems that plague our society is to raise people's self-esteem.

## Put away the stick

Trying to change a person's behavior by mentally or emotionally berating them, is like trying to fix a computer problem with a hammer. You would not even consider such an act, but we do this, without thinking, to the people in our lives.

Be careful what you say to others. Choose words that will encourage, rather than berate them. We can all work a little harder to raise our self-esteem and that of everyone that we encounter. One of the reasons that I am attracted to the coaching profession is because it is the aim of every professional coach to become our personal best and help others to do the same. By raising each other up we all benefit. It is possible to create a society in which everyone succeeds. We can create a win-win world.

A generation or two ago, many people believed that the way to improve someone's behavior was to mentally and emotionally abuse the person by belittling them and criticizing their actions. Unfortunately, there are some people who still believe this is an effective method. We know today that it is not. We know today that berating someone to try to improve their behavior, as I said before, is akin to hitting a computer with a hammer to make it perform better.

I remember coming home from grade school one day excited that I had received 85% on my report card in a particular subject, only to have my father ask, "Why didn't you get 95%?" Don't get me wrong, I'm not blaming him. He did what he thought was the best way to get me to improve. This was how he was raised and he was just doing what he thought was the right thing to do.

We know today that a better approach would have been for him to say, "That's great Jim. How might you improve even more next marking period?" This would have contributed to raising my self-image and increase the likelihood of my performing better in the future.

## Getting the best out of yourself and others

You probably realize by now that the way to bring out the best in yourself, or for that matter anyone else, is to minimize how you treat your mistakes and amplify your successes. Catch yourself, and others, doing things right. Be generous with your praise and stingy with criticism.

We've learned, over the years, that the best way to have a positive impact on performance is to focus on what a person is doing right. This, by the way, is in perfect alignment with what we learned earlier about the law of attraction.

One of the most effective weight loss programs in the world, Weight Watchers International, cheers people who have achieved any amount of weight loss, even one quarter or one half a pound. While this may not seem important when the person wants to lose 50 or 60 pounds, it is critical to encourage them to continue to follow the program. This is one of the reasons why this program has been so successful for so many years.

By celebrating even the smallest weight loss, the individual's self-image improves. They begin to see themselves succeeding in the program and it reinforces their commitment to continue. The small successes are what we need to achieve the big goal.

As I mentioned earlier, building people's self-esteem is something that is crucial for us to do more of in our society. If you want to learn more about this, I suggest that you contact the *National Association for Self-Esteem.* This is a great organization and I am proud to be a member. Its membership includes some of the top people in the field of self-esteem and human development.

With teenage suicide and drug abuse at an all time high, it is more important than ever to be helping our youth, and for that matter, everyone around us, to raise their self-esteem and feel better about who they are. The more we do this, the more we will improve our society.

## Energy vampires

In addition to the toxic people there is another group to avoid whenever possible. They are "energy vampires." You know the ones I mean. These are the people who leave you feeling emotionally drained after spending only four or five minutes talking with them. It's like they just suck the energy from you with all of their negativity and complaining. Since we are, in fact, affected by the energy around us, this is very real. If we stay in a negative situation for long periods of time, we will be affected by the negativity there.

Energy vampires include those people who can't wait to tell you about the latest disaster that you can do nothing to change, and will only cause you to feel bad if you let it. They are also those people who spend endless hours telling you about their latest surgeries and intimate medical details as if telling you is going to help, when in fact, all it does is drain more of your energy.

## Stick with the winners

I'm not suggesting that you be insensitive or unsympathetic to people who need someone to talk to, just that you minimize your interaction with those people, especially with those who do it constantly. You know who I'm talking about. There are people in all of our lives who, when we spend a little time with them, leave us feeling lousy, not even knowing why. It's because they literally suck the energy out of us.

If you want to have a happier and more fulfilling life and be more successful, hang out with people who are positive and support your dreams. One of the things that I learned when I first entered a program of recovery was to "stick with the winners." You stick close to those people who want to succeed at whatever they're doing and avoid the ones who want to live their lives complaining and sitting around moaning and groaning about their lot in life, doing nothing but depressing themselves and everyone around them.

## Attitude is everything

If you call my friend and colleague Jeff Keller on the telephone, you are greeted by an uplifting cheery voice who answers *Attitude is Everything.* You see, besides being his main philosophy in life, it is the name of his company and the title of his first book. Jeff is one of the people who I turn to when I'm feeling less than great, for he is always helpful and encouraging. He has been a great friend for many years and his message reminds all of us of the importance of our attitude in shaping who we become and what we accomplish in our lives.

A negative attitude not only makes a person unpleasant to be around, but robs them of their potential. Whenever we allow ourselves to slip into a negative attitude we take away our potential for problem solving. It is virtually impossible to be in a creative, resourceful state while in a negative state of mind. We literally do not have access to the power within us when we are negative. We shut off any possibility to succeed.

## A wonderful person but hard to be around

My mother-in-law, rest her soul, had a habit of looking at a situation or something on the news and saying "I feel so bad about _____." I doubt it is a coincidence that she spent the better part of her life unhappy and when asked how she felt, never replied "terrific." Be careful what you speak, think or say to yourself and others. Remember your subconscious mind, that part of your mind that is just beneath your waking state, does not know the difference between real and imaginary. If you continually say, "I feel bad . . ." you begin to feel bad. Like attracts like, it is a universal law. On the other hand, if you want to feel good most of the time, focus on the things that make you feel good. Tell yourself things that leave you feeling good. Use powerful questions like, "What am I happy about?," or "What is the best thing that happened to me today?" to cause you to feel even better.

Since it is impossible to feel grateful and indulge in self-pity at the same time, making a "gratitude list" or keeping a gratitude journal is the fastest way I know to, not only change how you feel, usually in minutes, but to immediately begin to attract more of the same to you. In other words, more things to be thankful for, which of course, are the feelings and experiences you want.

# 6

## IF YOU DON'T HAVE YOUR HEALTH ALL BETS ARE OFF

This is obviously one of the most important chapters in this book. After all, without your health, your life is not so much fun. Without your health your opportunities become quite limited. Without your health, living to a ripe old age becomes much less attractive.

The following information is not meant to replace qualified medical advice or treatment. If you are under the care of a physician or other medical professional do not make any changes to your health regimen without consulting them. I am not a doctor nor do I play one on television. Now that we have the legalese out of the way, let's talk about your health.

The information you read here is from the most reliable and trusted sources in the area of longevity and anti-aging medicine and includes many new, breakthrough treatments as well as age old remedies which have been proven to work.

You will also find information that may or may not have made it into the mainstream media. I urge you to do your own research before you take any information, here or anywhere else, as the truth. Your health is ultimately your own responsibility and your own business.

Much of what you read in this chapter will be based on my own firsthand experience as well as the latest longevity research. You will be reading excerpts from some of the medical professionals I feel are on the leading edge of health.

## How good can you feel?

Dr. Deepak Chopra has written about the idea of perfect health, and while this is probably quite possible, it is unlikely that most of us will achieve it. We can, however, aspire to what I call "ideal health." Ideal health is achieving the best state of health and fitness you are capable of achieving and maintaining your vigor as you age. As we discussed earlier, there are plenty of role models for living a fully productive disease free life for as long as we are alive.

In this chapter I will be introducing some new ideas from the forefront of the longevity movement. Some of these may challenge your beliefs and seem radical to you. As with anything you read, I don't ask that you agree with it or adopt my suggestions, just that you keep an open mind.

Too many people never have the kind of life they want and deserve simply because they run out of energy before they get where they are going.

Many people in our world today are in less than optimal health, however, much of this can be corrected with some simple lifestyle changes. Even people in countries that were once renowned for their health like Japan, Korea, China, Italy, and France, are now developing many of the debilitating diseases of the West due to the introduction of American fast food, with its high fat content and unhealthy ingredients, into these countries.

Most people's lifestyles in the twenty-first century do not include enough physical exercise and movement. Much of the physical labor of the past that provided us with a baseline of physical exercise has since been replaced by technology and modern conveniences in much of the developed world. Our youth are playing video games representing the sports their parents and grandparents used to play live. In America, a frightening percentage of our children are considered to be obese and the problem does not seem to be getting any better as our diets are increasingly comprised of fat, sugar and the biggest culprit of all — high fructose corn syrup.

All one needs to do is examine the typical shopping cart in a supermarket to see this problem clearly. America, I am saddened to say, is a nation of junk food eaters.

If you really want to make the rest of your life, the best of your life, developing a health plan is an important component. I encourage you to take charge of, and responsibility for, the state of your health and endeavor to achieve your optimal state of health and physical condition.

## My turning point

I was first introduced to the idea of health and nutrition by my friend Charlie Blackmore. I remember one day, while in my early 30's, saying to Charlie, "I feel awful. What can I do about it?" He said that if I placed my trust in him and followed his suggestions I would feel better. We were roommates at the time and I became a willing participant in his health experiment.

He began giving me large doses of several vitamins each day. I was introduced to things such as juicing, bee pollen, ginseng and numerous other (strange to this guy from New York City) substances. Charlie, a native of California, would spend countless hours browsing natural food stores.

Thus began my interest in health and nutrition. I have to honestly say that I believe that one of the reasons I survived my past lifestyle of excess was because aside from drinking and smoking heavily, I took good care of my health. Today, all things considered, I am quite healthy and steadily improving each day. Of course, I no longer drink or smoke and play an active part in assuring my future well being.

## A new model for a healthy life

In the past, in most cultures, people went to their family doctor when they were ill, and hopefully, did whatever he (most doctors were men) said. While this is still true for many people, there are two problems. One, people tend to expect the doctor to make them well without taking responsibility for their own health, and secondly, many people do not even follow their doctor's advice, expecting instead to be given a "magic pill."

I find it ludicrous that after one year, less than 30% of people are still taking the medicine their doctor prescribed. While I am not a big proponent of treating with pharmaceuticals, as you will read later in this chapter, I do feel that if I am seeing a doctor for help with a health issue, I should, at least, follow her advice, even if only until I can find a better way.

We are each responsible for our own health and well-being. It is unfair to our doctors to give them this responsibility. Like every other area of your life, if you want to have the power to change it, you must first be willing to take responsibility for it. When I began writing this book I was twenty-five pounds heavier than I am now. This was largely a result of slipping slowly back into some old eating habits and not exercising. I was responsible for having gained the extra weight, therefore, I knew I could lose it.

By the time this book was finished, I had lost the weight. I simply set a goal and wrote it in my journal. I then developed an action plan that, for me, included writing a food diary each day to keep track of what I was eating and eliminating some less-than-healthy foods from my diet. This, of course, was done over a period of time. If you try to make too many changes all at once, I think you're setting yourself up to fail.

I then increased my exercise and level of physical activity. It is interesting to note that the one common trait among people who have lost a significant amount of weight and kept it off is that they all maintained a food journal.

Approaching this from the prospective of *The Serenity Prayer* is probably a prudent idea:

*God grant me the serenity to accept the things that I cannot change.*
*Courage to change the things I can.*
*Wisdom to know the difference.*

## Serenity to accept the things I cannot change

There are undoubtedly many things about your health that you cannot change. Accept these but do not dwell on them. Of course, by the time you finish this book, what you believe you cannot change may be very different from what you now accept as your fate. Much of what people accept as "incurable illness" can, in fact, be eliminated with the proper approach. There are volumes of information and empirical evidence of people who have been cured of many illnesses that had been thought of as "incurable."

## Courage to change the things I can

This is the point of power as far as your health is concerned. Later I'll ask you to take a health and fitness inventory and explore what you can change about your present health conditions. Remember, our goal here is for you to achieve your personal best.

## Wisdom to know the difference

Permanent physical conditions are usually something that can not be changed later in life. It may improve greatly, but for the most part, only to a point. Injuries and such fall into this category.

On the other hand, many illnesses people suffer from can be virtually eliminated with the proper treatment. While this may sound contradictory to current mainstream medical beliefs, it is no less true. My wife, Georgia, had a mild case of arthritis in her thumb joint. Rather than see her suffer with it, or worse yet, become an aspirin addict, we explored a natural approach to eliminating it. There are many products on the market that have been used by people to virtually eliminate this condition completely.

Along with dietary changes, taking a supplement of Methylsulfonylmethane (MSM), Glucosamine and Chondroitin generally does the trick. As a matter of fact, MSM has been endorsed by actor Robert Culp as having helped him eliminate his arthritis problem completely, without the use of drugs.

I first started taking MSM more than a decade ago when my friend, Charlie (of course), one of the first people to be offering it for sale on the Internet, called me and suggested I begin taking it. Since Charlie has been my nutritional "guru" for over 30 years, I started taking it for my general health and have not stopped since. You may remember I mentioned earlier that Charlie was largely responsible for my remaining in reasonable health through all my years of abuse, and were it not for his knowledge of health and nutrition, I probably would have died from it all.

> *Disease cannot live in a healthy body.*
> — NORMAN WALKER

A lot of what you read here involves nutritional approaches to diseases which the pharmaceutical industry would like you to believe are incurable. Whenever I hear the word incurable, I think of something that was said by Norman Walker, the father of juicing, back in the 1970's. Walker who lived until he was ninety-nine and one half years old said simply, "disease cannot live in a healthy body."

## Healthy role models

As I have suggested before, finding role models who serve as guides to help you reach your goals is a great way to keep yourself motivated. For me, my good friend and attorney, Jim Sutton, is one of them. Jim is a marathon runner who works out at his gym six days a week and runs on the seventh. When I don't feel like exercising, all I have to do is think about him and it motivates me to get going. We all need role models. I figure if he has time to workout six or seven days a week, I can surely manage four or five.

One day at my health club, I spoke with one of the staff, a young woman named Leah Dillon. When she mentioned that she worked out almost every day I asked her how she got herself to do that since working out every day seemed pretty extreme to me. Her answer inspired me to begin seeing myself at a new level of fitness. She said, "I want to know what it would feel like, to be in the best physical condition of my life, just one time." Wow! What a concept. Inspired by her statement, I recently re-set my exercise goals.

## Achieving your personal best

Imagine achieving your own personal best with regard to health and fitness. How great would that be? I'm not talking about trying to fit into the media's idea of how you should look. I'm suggesting that you create *your* ideal body and *your* best health so that you can live your life filled with an abundance of health and energy.

## This is a clue to achieving health

Our creator has endowed us with a magnificent body that is capable of healing itself of virtually any ailment. Think about what happens when you cut your finger. Your body's systems go to work immediately to heal itself, with no drugs or intervention from you.

The reason the drug companies would like you to believe something is incurable is quite simple, profits, big profits!

Unfortunately, the business model of modern pharmaceutical companies is based on keeping people sick. Think about this, if I can get each and every person taking one or more drugs daily for life, I'd have a really good business going. The average American over the age of 55 is taking ten or more prescription drugs.

Interestingly enough, 11% of the population over 55 take no drugs whatsoever.

I want to make something clear. I am not anti-medicine, I am not anti-pharmaceuticals, I am not anti-anything when it comes to health, or anything else for that matter.

However, when the message from a drug company is something like the commercial that is currently running on television, the one that gives you the impression that if you take our "nifty little pill," you can gorge yourself at the buffet and eat everything that you want and not worry about it. I have a real problem with it. They are essentially saying you can eat everything in sight, because "our nifty little magic pill" will eliminate any heartburn or indigestion.

The reality is that everything comes with a price. You may mask the heartburn and indigestion much the way pain killers mask pain, however, neither does anything to eliminate the problem at the causal level.

In the case of the indigestion and heartburn, it's the diet that the person is eating, and if they continue to do that, they will pay a greater price at a later date.

One of my main arguments with the pharmaceutical industry is that they would like us to believe that by taking this magic pill everything will be fine; it won't. That's an absolute fact. Thinking this is so is akin to thinking that taking the battery out of your smoke detector will keep you safe from fire. You would not even consider such an absurd idea, but when it comes to our health, this is what we are being told, over and over again, to do.

## Your health team

In my opinion, life is not so much about how long we live, as it is our quality of life for however long we are on this earth. To achieve this, I have created a concept I call "My Health Team." Rather than put the responsibility for my life in the hands of my doctor, I have chosen to take personal responsibility for it and have assembled a team of health practitioners and advisors. You see, while I believe the medical profession, at least in the United States, is very good at treating illness and excellent at emergency medicine, I feel there is a big difference between not being sick and being healthy.

Many people in our world today might be considered "not

sick," since they have no overt symptoms and are feeling alright. However, that is not to say that they are healthy. While traditional medical doctors, for the most part, are great at helping you if you have an illness, it is not within the scope of their work to treat a well person. For this reason I have assembled my own team of health professionals.

Since I believe the one that is ultimately accountable for my health is me, I have appointed myself captain of my own health team. Depending upon your present level of health and fitness and your beliefs about the subject, your team members will vary from person to person. My own personal team includes, of course, our family doctor, and when necessary, one or more specialists, my dentist, and a doctor who specializes in longevity and preventive medicine.

At various times, my team will include a massage therapist, personal coach, chiropractor, personal trainer, yoga teacher, and various other modalities to help me stay balanced. By employing the concept of a "health team" I am able to maintain the best health possible and continue to improve as time goes on.

In addition to my health team, I eat a reasonably healthy diet and supplement that with a number of vitamins, herbs and some of the cutting edge nutrients like Co-enzyme Q10, a powerful antioxidant.

Stephen Sinatra, M.D., a board-certified cardiologist, a certified bioenergetic psychotherapist, a certified nutrition and anti-aging specialist, and the author of *The Sinatra Solution,* and co-author of *Reverse Heart Disease Now,* said that in his research, Co-enzyme Q10 was one of the greatest medical advances of the 20th century for the treatment of heart disease. And suggests what he calls his "Awesome Foursome" for maintaining heart health and treating chronic heart disease: magnesium, CoQ10, L-carnitine and D-ribose.

While they all do different jobs, he says, all support the production of ATP, the high energy molecule that fuels just about every physical activity in our body.

I exercise regularly, and as I said earlier, I've been inspired to set a goal of being in the best physical condition I have ever been. The interesting thing about this goal is that I can never reach it. It will keep moving as I approach it. The more fit I become, the more I increase my fitness capacity. This is one goal that I will enjoy never reaching.

One last thought about health and fitness. You may be thinking "I'm getting older; it's too late for me to get fit." Studies have shown that regardless of your age when you begin exercising, you can increase your fitness levels dramatically by following a regular exercise regimen. Of course, check with your healthcare provider before starting any exercise or nutritional program.

## Take charge of your health

Whatever changes you make to your diet and lifestyle, the

important thing to remember is to start taking responsibility for your health. If you want to have the life of your dreams, your physical and mental health are a significant part of it. Take charge of your health and fitness and make the rest of your life, the best of your life.

Set some specific goals right now to help you achieve your "personal best" level of health and fitness. Remember to check with your doctor or health practitioner before beginning any diet or exercise program, then develop your personal plan for achieving the level of health you want. Starting right now, plan to incorporate time each day for quiet time, prayer time, relaxation or meditation and make this part of your overall health plan.

## Action step — Your own health team

Think about your own health and fitness. What types of team members would help you become your personal best? Could a Yoga or Tai Chi teacher help you add more flexibility in your body? Would you benefit from the services of a personal trainer? When was the last time you had a physical examination? Men, in particular, tend to be very lax about this, as do certain ethnic groups such as my Irish relatives. Are your eating habits something that would benefit from a nutritional counselor? Could an herbologist be just what you need to help with a specific health issue?

In your journal, identify the members of your personal

health team, even if you do not presently know who they are. Just think about what kinds of specialties would help you achieve your health goals and live a healthier life, one filled with an abundance of energy.

## The new breed of doctor

Fortunately, there is a new breed of doctor emerging in the United States. These trailblazers are focusing on wellness rather than disease and treating people holistically. They draw from both traditional and complementary medicine and combine the best of both worlds. While traditional medicine falls quite short in treating causes of disease, focusing instead on treating symptoms, there is no better diagnostics in the world than the US medical system.

I find it interesting that many of these practitioners of preventive medicine and complementary healing modalities became interested in the field due to a personal crisis. When the doctors, themselves, became ill and realized the limitation of what they had learned in their medical training, they went looking for alternatives and were exposed to an entirely new way of looking at wellness.

The fields of preventive and longevity medicine are the fastest growing specialties in the United States due primarily to the fact that patients are no longer willing to accept being sick when they know that there are alternative approaches. On top of that, the access to information provided by the internet has spawned a new type of patient, one who is well informed and determined.

If you want to explore what might be available to you, I have listed some of these forward thinking doctors in the resource section in this book and on our Web site.

## My personal experience

My first encounter with this "new breed" of doctors was back in 1993. At the time, I was experiencing low energy to the point that I had to take a nap every afternoon. I knew instinctively that something was not right in my body, however, our family practitioner said I just needed to exercise more and that there was nothing medically wrong with me.

Not being one to give up easily, I kept seeking answers. My search led me to Dr. Ronald Hoffman founder of *The Hoffman Center* in New York City, so I immediately scheduled an appointment with him. After a lengthy interview, during which he asked me about my diet, health history, and lifestyle habits, he had a pretty good idea as to the cause of my troubles, however, wanting to be thorough, he ordered several tests including comprehensive blood work, and due to my past history, a chest x-ray and liver scan.

As he suspected from the start, my problem was an overgrowth of Candida, a yeast that can mimic over a hundred different symptoms. At the time, traditional medicine did not recognize this as a cause of illness. He prescribed a complete change in my diet, eliminating wheat and sugar and gave me homeopathic remedies to treat the Candida and suggested I add several vitamins that my blood work showed were lacking.

Within just a few weeks, I wrote in my journal "I do not ever remember feeling this good in my entire life!" My trouble was gone and I no longer needed daily naps. At that point, I was convinced that there is indeed a more intelligent way to approach health.

## Opposite approaches to the same problem

An example of the different approaches of traditional versus complementary medical doctors can be seen in their approach to treating Glaucoma, the second leading cause of blindness in the world and one whose risk typically increases with age.

The traditional practitioner will typically prescribe eye drops, surgery or a combination of the two and closely monitor the patient to ensure that the disease is not progressing. When I asked a leading ophthalmologist what may have caused my early stage Glaucoma, he shrugged his shoulders and said, "We don't know."

Not being one to accept that as a final answer, I turned back to the field of alternative medicine. Dr. Ronald Hoffman in his book *Intelligent Medicine* writes extensively on the subject and Dr. Joseph Mercola, in his email newsletter, offered an explanation of its causes as well as suggested simple changes to diet and exercise habits, combined with nutritional supplements like fish oil, lutein and zeaxanthin, to help prevent it or in the case of someone who already has this condition, to reduce the chance of it progressing.

Here is the root of the problem. If you were taught in medical school that there is no known cure for Glaucoma, or any illness for that matter, and you "believed" it (remember the chapter earlier about beliefs) you will probably look no further. This, by the way, is one of my pet peeves with traditional medicine. A doctor will tell a patient "nothing can be done about your condition." How arrogant!

Unfortunately, most people accept this (belief) as fact and leave the office depressed. In some cases, people even go home and prepare to die. This is a travesty.

A more accurate statement, one that would leave the patient some options would be for the doctor to say "There is nothing that *I know of* that can be done." This leaves open the possibility that there is something and may result in the person looking for and finding the cure. This by the way is happening all the time.

### Heavy metal is more than music

A few years ago I found my new doctor, Dr. Neil Rosen D.O. in Shrewsbury, NJ, another one of these new breed of doctor who specializes in preventive medicine. After a complete physical examination and battery of tests, including comprehensive blood work, I learned that I had abnormally high levels of lead in my body. As a matter of fact, my lead level was five times the upper limit set by the EPA.

If you take the time to investigate, you'll learn there are all sorts of nasty side effects of lead poisoning including Alzheimer's and heart disease. This may explain the absurd rise in Alzheimer's cases being reported each year.

Why don't we hear more about this? Simple, pharmaceutical companies  make billions of dollars from drugs which are designed to "treat" these diseases. The sad truth, at least in America, is that there is no profit to be made from a healthy population.

> *Unfortunately there is no profit to be made from a healthy population.*

The treatment for metal toxicity is pretty simple and runs the gamut from IV Chelation to taking nutritional compounds like Chlorella that bind to metals and flush them out. I am happy to report that my levels are back to normal and I feel fine. This experience and my natural curiosity about health lead me to investigate further. This is when I began to realize the scope of the toxicity problem.

## Long term solution

It's obvious that living a normal life, it's impossible to avoid these toxins, so what can we do? The solution I found and choose involves a combination of cleansing to rid my body of toxins and supplementing my diet with high quality nutrients.

## Strengthen your immune system

Below you'll learn about what I consider some of the leading health products available today and I'll share with you my own health regimen and some tips from many of the leading experts in the wellness field. Remember, if you are under a doctor's care, be sure to check with her or him before making any changes to your diet and health regimen.

However, and this is unfortunate, if you are in the United States and are going to a traditional medical doctor, chances are that they will not know about these things and even worse, will try to discredit them. A lot of this has to do with their bias toward the pharmaceutical industry.

Don't get me wrong, I'm not picking on your doctor, I am just pointing out how ill-informed they are when it comes to complementary medicine. I am not suggesting that you go against your doctors instructions, especially if you have a serious illness, but you owe it to yourself to investigate further.

Today there are more and more doctors employing complementary therapies and becoming more open and knowledgeable about holistic therapies. The fastest growing field in medicine, at least in the United States, is anti-aging or longevity medicine and many of these specialist are taking a preventive, holistic approach to wellness.

While we're on the subject of controversy, another area where my doctor and I had issues is in the use of Bioidentical Hormone Therapy. It was not so much that he was opposed to them, but that he did not know anything about them. Not being one to sit idly by, I investigated further and found several doctors who specialized in this and other preventive therapies.

Interestingly enough, the source I used to locate the doctor I chose, was the book *"Ageless"* by actress Suzanne Somers. Ms. Somers has done an amazing job of investigating anti-aging medicine and interviewed the top doctors in the world for her books, *"Ageless"and "Breakthrough."* While the big pharmaceutical companies have tried to ridicule her, pointing out that she is an actress not a doctor, they cannot argue with the credentials of her sources of information. The people she interviewed and quoted in her books are some of the leading physicians in the world.

If you want to remain healthy for the rest of your life, you owe it to yourself to learn about what's available in healthcare and not simply take the opinion of one individual as absolute fact.

As I said earlier, do not take anything that I write here as absolute fact either. While I am referencing some of the most highly regarded people in the wellness field, coupled with the latest research and my own personal experience, I urge you to take what works for you and leave the rest. It's your health and your life and you need to be the one who is in charge of it.

## Older adults' number one fear

If you ask aging adults which illness they fear most, Alzheimer's disease is likely to be at the top of the list, and for good reason: this devastating neurological condition slowly destroys people's ability to think while robbing them of their memory.

Alzheimer's is the most common cause of dementia in those aged 65 or older, and current statistics indicate that this debilitating condition affects more than 15 million people worldwide. With America's rapidly aging population—an estimated 30% of the US population will be 65 or older by the year 2050—it is projected that 14 million people in the US alone will be affected by Alzheimer's disease in the next few decades.

Having had experience with a family member with this dreaded illness, I can appreciate why it makes so many people concerned. While I believe there are precautions one can take like the aforementioned heavy metal testing and such, there are also some things you can do nutritionally to minimize the risks.

One of the most powerful brain nutrients I've found is Phatidylserine or "PS" for short. I first learned of this when, as I mentioned, I was doing research into Alzheimer's for personal reasons.

There have been more than 60 human studies and 3,000 scientific papers confirming the results of an Italian study that first discovered its value in treating Alzhemier's that found it not only prevented senile dementia and Alzhemier's but reversed the symptoms.

According to Dr. James Balch, author of *Prescription for Natural Healing*, "As long as you have plenty of PS in your bloodstream, your body automatically builds billions of vibrant, healthy new brain cells at any age." You can learn more about this powerful nutrient in our Web site's resource section.

## What leading edge docs have to say:

Many health advocates agree that gluten, found in most flours like wheat, rye and spelt, is a major cause of illness. *The New England Journal of Medicine* listed fifty-five diseases that can be caused by eating gluten, including many neurological diseases like anxiety, depression, dementia, schizophrenia, and migraines. Gluten has also been linked to autism. This is perhaps why, according to Mark Hyman, M.D., author of *The UltraMind Solution*, most, if not all, autistic children exhibit swollen brains as well as digestive disorders.

My candida problem, as mentioned earlier, was brought about by eating too much wheat and sugar. Dr's. Ronald Hoffman and Neil Rosen have both advised me to eliminate wheat from my diet, and while this is not an easy thing to do in our society, I am managing to adhere to it.

The result is that I not only feel better and have more energy, but I lost over twenty pounds in the process.

Dr. Mark Hyman also advises that in addition to eliminating gluten from your diet, you eliminate dairy, high fructose corn syrup and trans-fats. Doing this, he advises, will start you moving toward a healthier life.

Dr. Eric Braverman, author of *Younger You* and *The Edge Effect* and director of the Place for Total Health (PATH) Medical Centers in New York City advises people to go out and buy $50 worth of organic spices and $50 worth of organic teas. He points out that in herbal teas there are over four thousand anti-inflammatory flavonoids.

Leading edge, wellness orientated doctors point out that one of the leading causes of illness is inflammation, mainly due to our poor eating habits, and toxicity caused by any number of things, especially artificial sweeteners, food additives and pollutants.

For example, Dr. Russell Blaylock, a former brain surgeon and the author of *Excitotoxins- the taste that kills* and several other books cautions against the common practice of adding MSG (monosodium glutamate) to foods, including baby food, to enhance taste. MSG is an excitotoxin and is known to cause damage to our nervous system by causing our neurons to fire their impulses rapidly until they reach a state of exhaustion and die.

I find it unconscionable that our governmental regulatory agencies allow companies to call these excitotoxins by any name they choose and add them to our food as long as the glutamate content is less than 99 percent pure. This allows companies to use names like caseinate, chicken broth, and even "natural flavorings" to disguise these dangerous additives.

Hydrolyzed vegetable protein, an even more dangerous additive than MSG, contains three excitotoxins, and in many cases, added MSG. For a more detailed explanation of what takes place in the brain as a result of this, read Suzanne Somers interview with Dr. Russell Blaylock in chapter 14 in her eye opening book, *Breakthrough* or Dr. Blaylock's book, *Excitotoxins*.

Of course, this is not a total surprise when, by their own admission, the FDA is incapable of protecting the welfare of the people.

## Some things just need to be said

While I do not typically write about problems, much preferring to write about solutions, there is one exception I feel I need to make.

In the late 1970's, scientists Durk Pearson and Sandy Shaw wrote in their groundbreaking book, *Life Extension,* that one of the major problems with our health system in the United States was the Food and Drug Administration (FDA).

Here we are, some thirty-plus years later and the problem persists. Whether through incompetence, a misguided sense of their mission or kowtowing to the pharmaceutical industry, the FDAhas repeatedly allowed dangerous food and drugs to be marketed while making a major effort to block access to life saving treatments and nutritional substances, especially when they would threaten the profits of the drug industry. The time has come to put a stop to this.

The one and only organization who has, for the past three decades, fought to protect our rights and ensure access to healthy remedies is the *Life Extension Foundation*. I totally support their work and urge you to join this non-profit foundation to ensure that it continues. You can learn more about them on our resource page and Web site.

## Give exercise a chance

Thanks to my friend, Monika Kovacs for her exercise tips and suggestions. You can learn more about her in the resource section and on our Web site.

The human body is meant to be in motion at all times. Almost any form of regular physical activity: running, walking, biking, yoga, even something as simple as house cleaning or gardening provides tremendous benefits for our body and mind as we age.

It has been reported that adults who exercise frequently suffer less from cardiovascular disease and more likely live longer than those who do not. As little as 30 minutes of light exercise, like walking, three to five days a week, can potentially add over one year to one's life span.

To reap the most benefit from your exercise keep things

interesting and fun and team up with other fitness enthusi-asts. It has been proven that those who pair together and help keep each other on track, motivated, and challenged, will be more likely to stick to and succeed with a fitness program over the long haul.

Try exercises you've never done before; i.e. snow shoeing, hula-hoop, or even sign up for a belly dancing class.

Staying physically active also helps keep your brain more pli-able, maintain cognitive functioning and reduce memory loss.

Exercise produces endorphins and helps release stress from your body. Being physically active can simply make you feel better about yourself as you create a stronger, more flexible, and more capable you.

These simple to follow, practical, and effective steps can be integrated into anyone's daily life, so get up and start moving. Of course, as with any physical activity, be sure to check with your health professional before beginning.

## Stress and aging

We've all learned by now that chronic stress is bad for our health but just what does it have to do with aging? Scientists are finding it has a lot more effect than we thought.

Bruce McEwen, PhD, of Rockefeller University's Laboratory of Neuroendocrinology found that age may be more related to the presence of chronic stress and disease than to chronological age. In turn, moderating stress responses along with a healthy lifestyle can go a long way toward ensuring healthy aging.

Elissa S. Epel, PhD, of the University of California, San Francisco, reported that the decline in tissue builders such as growth hormone, testosterone, and estrogen, and an increase in cortisol, a hormone that reduces lean mass and bone density that is released in response to stress, may be responsible for some age-associated medical and psychiatric diseases. "Certain age-related changes can be modified with physical activity, sufficient sleep and good coping techniques," she observed.

Below, you'll find some simple actions you can take to improve your health and reduce the amount of stress in your life.

## Simple tips to stay healthy

In addition to establishing your personal health team and embarking on a regular exercise program, here are some other steps you can take to maintain and improve your health:

**Eat a well balanced diet**– I believe, and health experts will agree, that most foods can be eaten in moderation. Problems arise when people eat foods high in fat or sugar as the main component in their diet. Most Westerners eat way too much red meat, a habit that has managed to invade the otherwise healthy diets of Asian people as well, with the introduction of American food chains. While eating a small amount of red meat a couple of times a week is probably fine for the average person, eating large amounts of it contributes to high blood pressure, high cholesterol, and clogged arteries. Instead, add healthy servings of fish, especially wild salmon, rich in essential fats and oils, to your diet. Of course, eating large amounts of fresh fruits and vegetables is great, since they are packed with nutrients. Buying organic produce is a good idea whenever possible. Soy and whole grains are another good addition to our diets as they are high in protein and fiber and low in fat. The key to a healthy diet is quite simple, use common sense.

**Drink plenty of water–** The one thing every medical and health practitioner will agree on is that most people do not drink enough pure water. When I refer to water, I mean water, not coffee, tea or soda. While they contain water they are not perceived by the body as water and do not count. Drinking at least eight to ten glasses of water a day has many health benefits. Most physical therapists and chiropractors will tell you that many of their patients would have less back pain if only they drank more water. Water helps hydrate the disks between our spinal vertebrae, which can become dehydrated and cause pain. It also aids in digestion and helps flush toxins out of our bodies.

Virtually all weight loss programs emphasize the healthy benefits of water and the part it plays in maintaining a healthy weight. Personally I find it quite easy to drink a lot of water. I always have a large bottle with me at the health club and keep a big mug of water on my desk at home. Once you develop a habit of drinking plenty of water you will find that it is something your body wants and it becomes automatic. Adding a fresh lemon gives the water a pleasant taste and it adds the healthy benefits of the lemon, high in vitamin C and bioflavonoids.

**Water down your calories**– Here's an interesting tip from *Poland Spring Water:* A bottle of soda typically contains 140 calories while a bottle of water has zero. By replacing just one daily soda with water, you save more than 50,000 calories a year.

**Take time to breathe**– Most people breathe in a very shallow way. There is a wonderful breathing exercise by Andrew Weil M.D., author of the New York Times best seller, *Spontaneous Healing*. It is taken from Prana Yoga and is called the "relaxing breath."

Dr. Weil says, "It is the most powerful relaxation method he knows and one he teaches every patient that he works with."

Quite simply, you inhale through your nose quietly and exhale through your mouth. Begin by exhaling through your mouth completely, in order to empty your lungs of air. Next, inhale quietly through your nose for a count of four. Hold your breath for a count of seven and exhale through your mouth for a count of eight. What is important here is not the length of time, but the ratio four, seven, eight for the inhalation, holding, and exhalation.

**Here's how it's done:**

• Sit up straight

• Place the tip of your tongue up against the back of your front teeth. Keep it there through the entire breathing process

• Breathe in silently through your nose to the count of four

• Hold your breath to the count of seven

• Exhale through your mouth to the count of eight, making an audible "woosh" sound

That completes one full breath. Repeat the cycle another three times, for a total of four breaths.

You can do this exercise as frequently as you want throughout the day, but it's recommended you don't do more than four full breaths during the first month or so of practice. Later, you may work your way up to eight full breath cycles at a time.

Of course, if you are under the care of a medical doctor, please check with them before beginning this or any exercise. To reap the long term benefits of relaxing breath do a minimum of four cycles, twice a day. After a month you can increase the number of cycles to eight, but never do more than eight breath cycles. This is a very powerful technique and can have a profound affect on physiology.

*Caution: If you become out of breath or feel dizzy, stop.*

**Quiet time and relaxation–** Our entire society is on over-drive. People are rushing through their lives as though the goal was to get to the end, all the while missing the joy along the way. Happiness is a journey, not a destination. To have a full and rewarding life, we need to learn to enjoy every moment of it, not live for some far off future destination. One way to learn to slow the pace of your life in order to fully enjoy and appreciate it is to devote some time each day in quiet reflection, prayer and meditation. Spending time in quiet relaxation is one of the best things we can do for ourselves. Not only does it have enormous health benefits, helping to lower your heart rate and blood pressure, it's one of the keys to tapping into your creative potential.

When a person reaches the "alpha" state, a state associated with deep meditation, many events take place. This is the state associated with "waking sleep," when our brain is producing waves in the alpha range (4-8 Hz. per second) as opposed to our regular awake (beta) state of 10-15 Hz. per second and above.

In the alpha state, in addition to feeling calmer and being more relaxed, our bodies work more efficiently. Our internal healing mechanism is activated and our brain's ability to produce neuro-transmitter activity is increased. As an added benefit, the more we practice inducing this alpha state, the more our brain produces these frequencies on its own. This is one reason why meditation results in an overall reduction of stress.

*U.S. News & World Report*, December 26, 2005, reported the results of a study that found that the brains of people who meditated were five percent thicker in the areas that dealt with focus and memory than those of non-meditators. This implies that meditation actually improves attention span and memory.

While there are numerous books, audio programs and classes to help you learn meditation techniques and some of the audios I personally use are available from the resource page on our Web site, here's a simple technique to get you started.

- Sit quietly, where you will not be disturbed. Set aside fifteen to thirty minutes for this activity.

- Just relax and breathe as you normally would.

- On the in breath, feel your lungs filling with air.

- On the out breath, silently say the number "one" while exhaling slowly.

- Repeat this for fifteen minutes to begin and, as you become more comfortable doing it, stay for longer periods.

- If your thoughts wander, and they will, don't resist. Just gently bring your attention back to your breadth.

- Relax and enjoy the process.

## Reiki for stress reduction and relaxation

Another technique that I, and many others, have found beneficial is Reiki, a Japanese technique for stress reduction and relaxation.

The following is used with permission from the International Center for Reiki Training. Their contact information is listed in the resource section and on our Web site.

Reiki is administered by "laying on hands" and is based on the idea that an unseen "life force energy" flows through us and is what causes us to be alive. If one's "life force energy" is low, then we are more likely to get sick or feel stress, and if it is high, we are more capable of being happy and healthy.

The word Reiki is made of two Japanese words - Rei which means "God's Wisdom or the Higher Power" and Ki which is "life force energy." So Reiki is actually "spiritually guided life force energy."

Reiki treats the whole person including body, emotions, mind, and spirit creating many beneficial effects that include relaxation and feelings of peace, security, and wellbeing. Many have reported miraculous results.

Reiki is a simple, natural and safe method of spiritual healing and self-improvement that everyone can use. It has been effective in helping virtually every known illness and malady and always creates a beneficial effect. It also works in conjunction with all other medical or therapeutic techniques to relieve side effects and promote recovery.

While Reiki is spiritual in nature, it is not a religion. It has no dogma, and there is nothing you must believe in order to learn and use Reiki. In fact, Reiki is not dependent on belief at all and will work whether you believe in it or not. Because Reiki comes from God, many people find that using Reiki puts them more in touch with the experience of their religion rather than having only an intellectual concept of it.

While Reiki is not a religion, it is still important to live and act in a way that promotes harmony with others. Dr. Mikao Usui, the founder of the Reiki system of natural healing, recommended that one practice certain simple ethical ideals to promote peace and harmony, which are nearly universal across all cultures.

## Use it on everything

Emotional Freedom Technique (EFT) is a meridian based therapy developed by Gary Craig, based on the landmark discoveries of Dr. Richard Callahan. Dr. Callahan discovered that a person's fears and phobias could be treated by tapping on specific acupressure meridians.

I have been trained in EFT and have used it successfully with family members and in seminars, often with remarkable results. And many leading edge therapists are using EFT in conjunction with traditional modalities because of its ability to produce rapid results. Much of Craig's early work was in treating returning war veterans suffering from a variety of traumas.

The basic premise of EFT is that the cause of all negative emotion is a disruption in the body's energy system. The technique itself involves simply repeating a phrase that describes the problem, while at the same time, tapping a sequence of acupressure points on the body. I realize this sounds overly simple, however, I have personally witnessed extraordinary results.

If you'd like to know more about this, on our Web site's resource page there is a downloadable report, links to several of the leading EFT sites, and on our bonus page, you can download a sample EFT session about tapping for abundance, with my friend, Brad Yates. EFT is a simple and powerful technique anyone can learn and use.

# 7

## YOU DON'T HAVE TO EAT DOG
## FOOD UNLESS YOU WANT TO

On Jay Leno's late night talk show a while back, the host challenged the late actor and entrepreneur, Paul Newman, to eat some of his own dog food as a way of demonstrating his claim that it is a healthy natural food. Not willing to be up-staged, Newman ate the dog food on network TV. His demonstration was by choice however.

The sad truth is that large numbers of older people in the United States are eating pet food and other low cost foods because they can not afford to do anything else. According to the Social Security Administration, 46% of people over the age of 65 have income below the poverty line.

This is absurd in a country where wealth abounds. My

heartfelt wish for you is that you never experience this and the purpose of this chapter is to provide you with some specific ideas and information so that you never have to live this way. It continues to amaze me that at least in the United States, it is possible to be awarded a college degree, even an advanced degree and not ever learn about the workings of our financial system. A majority of college students recently questioned, did not know the difference between an asset and a liability.

Our educational system falls quite short of preparing their graduates to live in the real world. This is something that fortunately many of us are working to change.

## You deserve pampering too

The other day my wife, Georgia, was at our local beauty salon for a visit. Ever since I've known her, Georgia has had regular manicures, pedicures, facials and other personal care services. She takes great care of herself and it shows.

Sitting next to her was a woman who appeared to be in her late 60's or early 70's who was also getting a pedicure. In talking with the woman, Georgia learned that this was the first time she was doing this and only because someone gave her a gift certificate.

The woman went on to explain to Georgia how she and her husband were "retired" and living on his meager pension and social security. "I would never splurge on something like this!" she said, "We don't even go out to dinner very often and only go to the movies if it's a matinee. I even clip supermarket coupons each week to save money."

Please don't misunderstand, I see nothing wrong or embarrassing about not being able to afford certain luxuries. I have, at more than one point in my life, barely been able to afford to eat. However, to see people who worked hard all their lives being forced to live this way, is a travesty.

Here they are, after a lifetime of labor, scrimping and scraping just to get by in one of the wealthiest societies in the world. This struggle is not because they are lazy, after all, the man worked all of his life. No, it is because they did not take the time to learn about finances and have accepted the myth that once you retire, your income producing days are over.

## You can learn about money

Robert Kiyosaki, author of the *Rich Dad* series of books, nailed it when he said "People will spend 50 or 60 hours a week earning money, but are unwilling to invest 2 or 3 hours learning how to manage it."

I am not a financial expert by any means, however, I invest countless hours reading books and listening to audio programs written by experts in this field. In the resource section on our Web site you'll find a list of some of the books and other resources that can help you in this important area.

Money and finance is no different than any other field and

can be learned by anyone who can read. You do not have to be a CPA or professional investor to understand the basics of how money works. You can easily learn enough to formulate your own plan. While experts abound, having your own plan is the first step in taking charge of your financial future.

For example, in Georgia's brief conversation with the woman at the salon, she learned that she and her husband sold their big house because they were tired of maintaining it. They then bought a town house with the cash. From what I've learned, there are several things they could have done differently that would have given them the same result but with more disposable income.

For one, they may have been able to rent their house, borrowed against some of the equity, purchased the town house and been left with extra money to put in another income producing investment.

If you're one of those people who would like to continue earning income or want to do a little something extra for more money, the following pages outline just a few of the many opportunities that exist for anyone who would like to have more money in their life.

While it is not within the scope of this book to provide you with an education in finance, I would like to devote some time and space to a brief discussion of the subject and how you can help yourself become more financially secure, and ultimately, financially independent. Finances are the greatest source of stress in people's lives and are probably responsible for more marital relationship problems than anything else. Money is a core issue in our society among everyone regardless of their income level.

I've always liked the principle I learned from Robert Kiyosaki and Sharon Lechter regarding finance. They call it "getting out of the rat race." If you really want to learn more about this topic, I highly recommend reading the *Rich Dad, Poor Dad* series of books. It will change your perspective about wealth and money. Being out of the "rat race" means that you have sufficient passive income to support your lifestyle and pay all of your expenses. This is income you receive whether or not you actively work. In other words, having residual, asset, or royalty income to support your lifestyle. This gives you the freedom to pursue whatever it is you want to pursue in life.

## A painful lesson

Several years ago I learned two very valuable lessons about finances. It was during the dot com boom and I had invested money in a high-technology stock, which I purchased for $53 a share. Fortunately for me, I did not purchase a lot of it, so while the lesson was an expensive one, it was not devastating. I sat one day as the stock reached $65 a share and a little voice inside of me suggested, "This would be a good time to sell it, take my profit and go do something else with the money."

Before I could act on that small voice within, the one we generally consider to be our intuition or instinct (and the one that is usually accurate), another little voice, this time from my head (which I will label my greedy voice) said, "Hold on, it may go even higher." That was on a Tuesday morning, and that particular stock started to go steadily down from $65 a share until it finally bottomed-out, or more accurately, I got out at $1.50 a share, losing a considerable amount of money along the way.

## Learn from your mistakes

I learned two very valuable lessons from this experience. The first lesson was to trust my instincts and not let greed get in my way. My first instinct was correct, one which would have allowed me to get out with a profit.

The second lesson, which is even more important, is to not go into things that I do not fully understand. While I have a cursory knowledge of the stock market, I don't consider myself to be an expert. If and when I ever go into stock investing again, I will have gained the expertise necessary to make it profitable.

Like any other industry, the stock market works with specialized information and the people that understand it and know how to play the game make money.

## Raise your means

Another financial author's work I admire is Suze Orman. She wrote *The Courage to be Rich* and a series of financial books. My only challenge with Suzy is that part of her plan is to cut back on your expenses by drinking cheaper coffee and having less personal services. I personally don't like that concept. I much prefer the Kiyosaki model, which is "Live within your means and raise your means." That suits

> *Live within your means and raise your means.*
>
> — ROBERT KIYOSAKI

me and my lifestyle much better. I enjoy the finer things that this life has to offer and why shouldn't I? And why shouldn't you for that matter?

## Create assets

One of Kiyosaki's metaphors struck me as if someone had dropped a brick on my head, because it was so simple and so obvious. If you're not starting with a lot of money and are, like most people, working for a living, the way to create wealth is to create assets that will produce income. This income can then be used to purchase other assets and liabilities. A liability, in his view, is something that costs you money rather than provides it. Things like cars, boats, airplanes, and jewelry, are liabilities. His suggestion is to delay buying expensive luxuries until you can pay for them with asset income. This way, you are not buying liabilities with your labor.

## Your financial future

One sure way to financial freedom is owning your own business, even if it's only part-time. If you look at the statistics of self-made millionaires, you'll discover that the majority of them are small business owners and the tax system in most nations is set-up to aid the small business owner since they create jobs for the rest of the population.

In today's uncertain employment climate, it is more important than ever to have a measure of control over your income, and being an independent business owner is one of the best ways to accomplish this. The average family would be living better, with less stress, and more enjoyment if they earned an extra few hundred dollars a month. This can easily be accomplished by owning your own part-time business.

Aside from the financial rewards of your own business you gain peace of mind and a sense of security knowing that no matter what, you have some control over your income. If something were to suddenly happen to your job you would at least have something to fall back on. With so many companies downsizing today, this is more important than ever.

Whether you're presently employed or retired, beginning a part or full time business s is one of the best financial moves you can make.

## Independent business owner (IBO)

While I may be able to write books to create assets, what do you do if you're not a writer? There are several other options. You could buy an existing business, start one from scratch or become a franchise owner. Another avenue to owning your own business is in the direct sales or network marketing industry.

I personally like this option for those people who are either just starting out as an independent business owner or who want to be able to start part-time, while maintaining a full time job, professional practice, or even a traditional business.

Network marketing is one of the few industries that you can go into with little or no money and become, if you have the desire and the drive, independently wealthy.

What makes network marketing attractive to many people is its low barrier to entry and its people to people method of distribution. If you so choose, you can build a sizeable network of independent distributors, known as your "downline," from which you receive override commissions. The cost of joining your typical network marketing company is less than $100.

Typically, a person is drawn to a particular company for their products or services. You discover a nutritional or weight loss product, for example, and after taking it for a while and realizing the benefits from it, you decide to join the company as a distributor and begin selling it. The advantage to this type of business model is that the people selling the products are also customers, and as such, become a "product of the product." This provides real credibility to the products.

I know several people, including Jimmy Smith who you read about earlier, who are multi-millionaires today, having started with nothing more than a burning desire to succeed in network marketing. And in Jimmy's case, he was sixty-two when he did it!

## The new rich

It is believed by experts that a high percentage of the 10 million new millionaires that will emerge over the next decade will come from the ranks of the network marketing industry.

This prediction becomes obvious when one considers how many people are opting out of corporate careers with their long hours, uncertainty, and unrealistic demands, and moving toward home-based businesses. People who want a better quality of life and the freedom to choose where they work and when are drawn to network marketing, and the advent of the Internet has made this easier than ever.

## A true twenty-first century business

Network marketing is essentially a method of product distribution which allows an individual distributor to resell a line of products or services while at the same time compensating them for introducing other people into the business. This P2P (person-to-person) selling system is a leading twenty-first century distribution model, being endorsed by notable business leaders like Warren Buffet and Robert Kiyosaki and embraced by forward thinking entrepreneurs from all walks of life.

Today's network marketing companies are attracting the best and the brightest from the ranks of disgruntled and downsized corporate executives, time-stretched professionals, and everyday people who want an additional income stream.

That said, if you feel attracted to network marketing as a way of adding additional income, and I highly suggest you do so, since having multiple streams of income is one of the most prudent strategies for financial security, there are some things you'll want to consider in making your choice from among the hundreds of network marketing companies.

In my opinion the most important criteria is to find a product or service that you are absolutely passionate about. It is important to be passionate about what you're doing. If you're not, do something else.

What has made the direct sales industry such a huge success, aside from the potential to literally earn a fortune, is the method in which they sell. Typically, a person learns about a product from a friend or acquaintance, becomes a customer and begins enjoying the benefits of the product. They are then offered the opportunity to become a distributor.

Another significant benefit to network marketing is that distributors are following a tried and true, proven system. This makes it easy for the novice to get up and running quickly, even with no prior business experience.

The parent company handles all the details of product fulfillment, administration, etc., and most enable the distributor to set up their own private labeled Web site to send people who would like to learn more or order online.

In addition to finding a product that you love, make sure that you feel good about the company. If possible meet the top management.

## Global opportunity

Many US network marketing companies have done exceptionally well in other countries, where the hand to hand selling model fits well into the culture of the country. The closely knit community structures in Asia and other countries for example are well suited to the person to person business model. Various experts claim that in the future, a very high percentage of goods and services will be sold by direct sales companies.

A side benefit to network marketing is that you generally get to meet and hang out with some very positive and highly motivated people.

As my friend and hero, the late Charlie "Tremendous" Jones said, "You are today what you will be five years from now, except for the people you meet and the books you read." Being around people at network marketing gatherings is a good way to immerse yourself in positive energy on a regular basis.

## If you decide networking marketing is for you:

• Find a company whose products you like and would buy even if you were not in the business.

• Check out the company to make sure their values and mission is in alignment with your own.

• Choose a sponsor who will be supportive and will be willing to help you get started.

• Find a mentor and follow their system.

• Be patient and stick with it. It may be slow going at first, however, patience and persistence will pay off for you in the long run.

• Above all have fun; not only will it make you feel good, but you will attract a lot more people by making your business fun.

## Becoming debt free

No discussion on finance would be complete without at least a mention about debt and the problems it can cause. I know this first hand because I have had more than my share of it and have spent a period of time eliminating the debt in my life.

I suggest to anyone who wants to have a stress free life —— especially if you want to be financially independent — that you make it a priority to reduce the debt that you have and not incur any new debt.

One of the ways to do this is to take the amount of money that you can afford to pay each month on your total debt and divide it by the number of credit cards you have. Then, make the minimum payment on every card other than the card with the highest interest rate. Pay the remainder of your budget on that card until it is paid off. Then move on to the next highest rate card, and so on.

This very simple debt reduction system, is taught by *Debtors Anonymous* and every other program that helps people get out of debt. I will say here that if you are deeply in debt, that you get some help. Find some agency or group that can help you learn to manage your debt.

Many people are deeply in debt because of a gambling problem. If this is your case, by all means get professional help; go to *Gamblers Anonymous*. Gambling is a serious illness like alcoholism and drug addiction and needs to be treated as such. If you feel that you have a problem, do something about it. Don't let it destroy your life.

For more ideas, resources and links to financial services, be sure to visit the resource page on our Web site.

## Appreciate the abundance you already have

Often we do not even notice the abundance that we already have in our lives. We tend to forget all the little signs that the Universe is, in fact, supporting us. One way to begin to see and appreciate the abundance that is flowing into your life, and a way to attract more, is to start keeping an evidence journal. An evidence journal is simply a running record of any money that comes into your life. If you receive a gift of money, record it in your journal. If you find a small amount of money on the street, write that in your evidence journal, too.

Doing this serves several purposes. For one, it draws your attention to the abundance that you are receiving, thereby creating a feeling of gratitude. And it serves as a sign that you are in fact increasing your wealth. This can be likened to a ship at sea. When land approaches, the ship begins to see driftwood floating in the water. The driftwood is a sign that land is close by. If you just started a new business you will not see the financial rewards for a time, however, by recording any amounts of money you receive you will be noticing the "driftwood." Remember, we get more of what we focus upon. If you want more money notice the money that you are already receiving. Something else that I like about keeping an evidence journal is that I can look back at it and see just how fortunate I am and how much the Universe has supported me. This always makes me feel better.

## Your change box

One of the ideas that I've implemented from Suze Orman's *Courage to be Rich* book is to begin collecting change. Whenever I purchase something, I always use paper money, even though I may have coins in my pocket. At the end of the day I deposit these coins into a change box that I keep in my dresser. When the box is filled I take it to the bank and cash it in. I then take the money, usually around $100, and buy something nice for myself or my wife, or donate it to a worthwhile charity. Sometimes we use the money to go out to a nice restaurant. By saving the coins each day, I do not even notice the amount of money as it builds into a small nest egg. I know of people who do this for an entire year and use the collected coins to pay for a family vacation. After all, if you did this for a year, at the end you would have about $1,200 which could pay for a short vacation for you and your family.

## Keep a spending record

Have you ever looked into your wallet or handbag at the end of the day and wondered where the money went? I know I have. We tend to go through our day purchasing items like newspapers, coffee, tea, magazines, candy, soft drinks, snacks etc., without giving much thought to it.

If you really want to gain a sense of where your money goes, you may want to use a spending record. What this means is that for one month you record every purchase you make regardless of its size. Get a small pad or use your PDA and keep a running record of each and every purchase you make throughout the day.

When I first did this exercise, I was amazed at how much I spent on insignificant items. Keeping a spending record for a month or two is a great way to gain control over your spending.

The idea of this exercise is not so much to cut spending as it is to make you more aware of where your money goes. Once you know this, you are then in a better position to decide what you want to do with your money and whether or not you want to change some of your spending habits.

## Discuss finances openly

In completing this chapter about finances, I would like to offer a suggestion. Talk openly about money and finances with your family. Had more of us learned about money and finances growing up, we would have been better equipped for the world that lay ahead.

I don't know about you, but the only references I ever heard about money growing up were that other people had more than we did and that there was never enough. These and other negative messages given to young people sets them up for financial struggle, or at best, a poor understanding about how money works.

It is interesting to note that wealthy people begin educating their children about money at a young age. These young people become astute financial stewards by the time they're adults and are able to manage and secure their own financial future.

Although most of the messages that I received about money growing up were negative, I did learn some positive ones. I learned that if I was willing to work for it, I could earn pretty much what I wanted.

Since money to me as a young person meant independence and freedom, I found ways to earn whatever money I needed. As a teenager I was doing quite well financially.

A side benefit to this was that I discovered that I could easily learn new tasks. Both of these beliefs, created in my early teens, have served me well over the years.

Taking the time now to teach your children about finances will go a long way toward ensuring their financial success.

# 8

## SIMPLE STEPS TO ENHANCE YOUR LIFE

The following chapter is designed to introduce you to ideas, practices and techniques which I have found helpful. As with everything else in this book, have fun with it, use what works for you and leave the rest.

### Start your day off right

In my first book, *Handbook to a Happier Life*, I wrote about a technique I call "Morning Questions." The premise is quite simple. Most people, when they wake up in the morning, begin their day with what I like to refer to as "stupid questions." They ask themselves questions that typically have no answer and only serve to make them feel bad. For example, asking, "Why do I have to get up so early?" will do nothing to help you feel good about your day.

On the other hand, asking yourself questions like, "What am I looking forward to today?" or "What am I grateful for in my life?" will shift your attention, and hence, your emotions, in a positive, more empowering direction.

I challenge you to make up a series of two or three questions that, when answered, will help you begin your day on a positive note. Instead of jumping out of bed first thing in the morning, give yourself a minute or two to ask and answer these questions. Do this for thirty days and then decide if, in fact, you feel better and want to keep doing it.

## Extraordinary self-care day

When was the last time you took a day just for yourself? I first learned the principal of an "Extraordinary Self-care Day" at a workshop given by my friend, Terri Levine, the author of *Work Yourself Happy*. Essentially an "Extraordinary Self-care Day" means taking one 24-hour period where you take exceptional care of yourself. You do no work at all. I know, I can hear your protest. I protested too when I first heard this idea.

"But you don't understand, I have to check my voicemail, I have to return phone calls, I have to answer my emails" and on and on. The truth is any of us can take a day for ourselves without consequence. Believe it or not, the world will keep spinning. Calls will wait and so will email.

This is a day just for you. If you normally do the cooking, on your extraordinary self-care day, you will refrain from making meals. Trust me, your family will not starve. Obviously, if there are others who depend on you, you would have to modify this. Perhaps you can have someone take over your duties for this one day.

Overall, try to do nothing that is related to your normal work. This is a pampering day just for you.

The first time I did this, I discovered just how my work relates to things that I do on any given day. Most of my reading was centered on business topics. Being an entrepreneur and self-employed, I was convinced I had to be working all the time. I was wrong. Kicking and screaming, I embarked on my extraordinary self-care day. I took a walk, read part of a novel, took a luxurious bath in our soaking tub (something I never used to do) and just relaxed and took extraordinary care of myself. What a concept!

It's been a few years now and my extraordinary self-care day has become an integral part of my life. I not only feel better and am having more fun, I have my life back. Doing this regularly has enabled me to put my work back into perspective. I no longer work seven days a week and I no longer do email throughout the day.

The interesting thing is that because of my taking this time to nurture myself, I'm actually more productive. Because I'm taking better care of myself I have more clarity and I'm able to better focus on the task at hand. Because I am taking better care of myself, I am more creative. Most of all, because I am taking better care of myself, I feel better and am happier. After all, isn't that what it's all about?

## Action step — Your extraordinary self-care day

Schedule one 24-hour period, some time within the next 10 days, when you can give yourself an extraordinary self-care day. Once you've done this, see how you might be able to do this weekly and when you feel really ready, schedule an extraordinary self-care day for what would have been a normal work day.

Write a list of some of the things you'd like to do but have been putting off because you are "too busy." It may be something simple like getting a massage, visiting a park, or buying an ice cream cone. Perhaps it's spending an entire day at a luxury spa. Yes, men, you can do this too.

## What's working?

Each week my wife and I sit down and complete a simple exercise I learned from the book, *Breaking the Rules* by Kurt Wright. In this book he uses a questioning process that I feel is truly brilliant in its ability to focus a person's attention in the direction that they want to go. Georgia and I use the first question, "What's working?" as a way to shift our focus away from anything that may not be quite right and towards those things that are working. We write a list of everything we can think of that is going right. Sometimes it's a short list, but more often it's quite long and filled with exciting opportunities.

Doing this accomplishes two very important things. First it leaves us feeling good about what we are doing. Often people are focused on the things that are not working and they wonder why they are depressed.

As we each discuss and write out what is going right, we automatically begin to feel better. This in turn attracts more of that to us. Remember that you get more of what you focus upon. This is the law of attraction. Like attracts like. So if you are consistently focusing on what is going right, you will see more of that and begin to attract more of the same.

Let's delve a little further into how you can use this for any area of your life. As I have said before, I work on steadily improving my health, however, there are times when I feel that I am not making as much progress as I would like or times when I have slacked off on my fitness program. When this happens I'll do a "What's working?" exercise for my health. I will begin listing all the things that I am doing that are moving me towards my goal of ideal health.

My particular list may include things such as going to the health club four or five days a week, following a balanced food program, eliminating caffeine, reducing sugar, taking a yoga class, seeing my nutritionist, having a massage and so on. No matter how long or short my list is at any particular time, it causes me to focus my attention on those things that are working, which causes me to feel better and moves me further along toward my goal.

This one simple question can be used in any situation for any part of your life. You can use it with your spouse, children or co-workers. If you use this in a business situation, be prepared to see some strange expressions on the faces of your co-workers. We have become so conditioned to asking the exact opposite that just asking the question stops people in their tracks.

## The face in the mirror

In my second book, *This is Your Life, Not a Dress Rehearsal*, I wrote about the idea of verbalizing your affirmations while looking into a mirror. This is a powerful technique that can speed your progress, however, approach it with caution. If you're new to personal development work, jumping into doing mirror work can be a bit intimidating. When you recite an affirmation, especially one that deals with your self-image or self-esteem issues, the intensity of looking deep into your eyes can create some uncomfortable feelings.

I don't mean to scare you away from doing this, but I want you to know that you may surface some feelings and emotions that you have forgotten about.

Years ago, I used a mirror exercise as part of my live workshops but soon stopped doing it when I realized it made people uncomfortable, especially since they were doing it in a group setting. Mirror work is something that you want to do in the privacy of your own home.

A great phrase to begin your affirmation work is, *I approve of myself.* I learned this from Louise Hay many years ago and it became the catalyst that triggered significant positive changes in my life and helped lead me to where I am today.

While doing this affirmation, facing into a mirror was a bit challenging at first, I kept at it. Today I have absolutely no problem looking myself straight in the eye and saying, "I approve of myself." It's simple for me to do this now, because I do approve of and accept myself.

I believe that a lack of acceptance or approval of ourselves, not to mention self-love, is the root cause of many of the problems that people face in creating a life filled with the joy and abundance that they deserve.

If you verbalize your affirmations while looking deeply into your own eyes, you will soon notice that you are making small positive shifts in your life. For me this was the beginning of my smoking cessation, and as I mentioned, the beginning of my making many positive changes in my life.

Please remember that personal development work is much like peeling the layers of an onion, so take your time and be gentle with yourself. If at any time you feel too uncomfortable or anxious, by all means seek professional assistance. Doctors, therapists, counselors, coaches and myriad others in the helping profession are there to assist you in your journey to make the rest of your life, the best of your life.

## Your treasure map — a visual guide

My first introduction to the concept of treasure maps was when I was living in San Francisco, back in 1977. I was visiting the new apartment of a friend in Mill Valley, a lovely, picturesque town in Marin County. She had just moved into a delightful studio apartment that was exactly what she always wanted and included an amazing view of the Golden Gate Bridge and the San Francisco skyline. It was the kind of view you usually see on post cards.

What convinced me of the value of using treasure maps to help a person manifest their desires, was seeing my friend's treasure map on her wall. Looking at her visual, complete with a photo of herself, local real estate ads, pictures of the San Francisco Bay, her positive affirmations, and so on, I could not help but notice that the photos in her treasure map were the *exact* scene I was seeing out her window. It sent a chill up my spine when I saw how closely her actual home matched her dream.

If you've seen the immensely popular law of attraction movie, *The Secret,* or read the book, you may remember hearing about "dream boards." They are essentially the same thing as a "treasure map." To my knowledge, the idea was first introduced by Shakti Gawain in her best seller, *Creative Visualization,* published in 1975 by New World Library, which happens to be the current publisher of *Handbook to a Happier Life.*

Although I had been exposed to the idea, it wasn't until I

was beginning to put my life back together that I started using treasure maps to help me achieve my goals.

At the time I owned a beat up old car. Actually that is an understatement. It was a twelve year old hunk of metal that barely ran. It had a vinyl top, but most of the vinyl was worn away and what was left was peeling. There was a hole in the floor on the driver's side that let cold wind in during the winter. I used to place my foot over it. The paint was fading and it did not run very well.

My wife, who I was dating at the time, did not even want to ride in it. So whenever we went out we took her late model luxury car.

My goal, back then, was a new, Honda Accord EX. Knowing about the power of treasure maps, I had visited the Honda Dealer and obtained a brochure of the car I wanted. In addition to having a written goal of driving the new Honda, I placed a picture on the wall above my desk where I would see it throughout the day.

One day I took the picture down because the car was in my driveway. I owned a new Accord.

Please do not misunderstand, I am not suggesting that this just happened by itself. The car dealer did not drive by my house looking for someone to give the car to. I had to do certain things to improve my life to be in a position to make it possible, but the treasure map helped speed things up by consistently imprinting on my mind that which I wanted.

If you want a new car, an even better technique is to visit a dealership and have someone take a photo of you sitting in the car of your dreams.

Whatever you want to have in your life, use visuals to help your subconscious learn what it is that you want. For example, if you want to go on a fabulous vacation to Hawaii, get some travel brochures and make a collage of the pictures of beach scenes, hotels, and other images that will give you visual reinforcement for your goal.

When we were looking for our home in Bucks County, Pennsylvania, I created a treasure map using a picture of Georgia and myself, pictures of Bucks County, a headline that said "Bucks County Pennsylvania," ads for homes, and a picture of the kind of house we wanted. I wrote phrases and affirmations on it as well and hung it where we would see it daily. This helped reinforce our goal in our minds and helped bring it to us faster.

Visual aids are very powerful, if you doubt this just look at the impact television has had on people's buying habits. The next time you look at a magazine, notice how much more powerful the ads with photos are as compared to those with just text. You too can use the power of visual imagery to help you obtain what you want.

## Put your dreams in a box

Another variation along the same line as a treasure map is

something called a creation box. I learned this from the writings of Jerry and Esther Hicks, authors of the *Law of Attraction* based series of books.

To use this idea, simply obtain a box of whatever size you feel is appropriate. As you read through newspapers, magazines and catalogues, notice the pictures of the things that you would like to attract into your own life. They may be material things, like cameras, DVD's computers, automobiles, new furniture, or they can be emotional states like joy, peace and serenity. When you see a picture, particularly something that you would like to have, a place you would like to visit or an emotional state that you would like to experience, cut it out, and after looking at it closely, place it in your creation box. You can even write on slips of paper things that you want to have or emotional states that you would like to experience more regularly.

As with the treasure map you are once again teaching your conscious and subconscious mind what you would like to have or experience in your life. You are, in effect, actively creating your life as you live it.

Our subconscious mind records everything that occurs in our lives. This has been validated using hypnosis. People who have been hypnotized have been able to recall many years in the past with great detail. Your subconscious mind will record and remember the fact that you chose specific things and affirmed your desire to have them in your life. This will reinforce your intention and help you move more quickly toward your desires.

From time to time you can revisit your creation box to reinforce these ideas. I have found, over time, that when I go back to look at my creation box, I already have many of my desires in my life. It all happened as if by magic!

## Making the most of your time

I'm certain that you will agree that we all live very busy lives. Most of us are living a hectic pace and it's all we can do just to keep up with the demands placed upon us by modern living. Many couples are balancing careers or businesses with raising families and caring for their children and older parents, while at the same time trying to find a little time for themselves. Add to this, time for running household errands, shopping for groceries and many other tasks we all do to keep our lives moving along, and it can be overwhelming.

We have friends who, in addition to their own high-powered careers, are raising two teenagers. With all the activities available to today's teens, just keeping up with them is almost a full-time job. Another friend of ours has a fourteen year old son, who plays nine different sports, each with its own practice and game schedule, not to mention equipment. So how do we not only cope and maintain balance, but even thrive in all of this?

I believe, and there is plenty of empirical evidence to support it, that time management and preplanning is the key. The time that you devote to planning your week and day will pay for itself many times over.

Whether you use a notebook or journal, paper based planner, or personal digital assistant, it is crucial to your success and well-being to invest time in planning your activities. I noticed when I began adding my exercise time to my daily plan that, instead of trying to squeeze it in as I went along, I was there at the appointed time and on track to reach my fitness goals.

I even schedule time to go out with my wife on a "date." This has become increasingly important as I become busier and am asked to do more public speaking. By scheduling our "date night," usually a Friday, I know I will not, if at all possible, make any other commitments. If I do, I will schedule our date on another evening. Often the things that are most important to us tend to become squeezed into whatever time is left over. We lose out on the things that we most want to do as a result of not planning our day.

Awhile back I noticed that my writing time, something that for me is the most important activity and the one I enjoy most, was being relegated to "fit in" where possible. I began scheduling one hour a day to write. As a result I have become even more productive and am enjoying it more.

One of the secrets to a balanced life I learned from my friend, Jim Sutton. When I asked him how he managed to be exercising every morning, being an attorney with a very busy practice, he replied, "I make it one of my top three things to do each day." Note he did not say one of my top ten. By putting the really important activities on your schedule first, you will ensure they're being completed. If you take care of the "big rocks" first, you can always find the time for the smaller ones.

What are your most important three to five daily tasks and activities? For me writing and exercise are scheduled first, I then look at my other tasks and schedule time for the other top two or three. In the remaining time I do the less important things that we all need to do.

When you look at your weekly or monthly plan, do you see time for self-care and relaxation? If not, ask yourself if this is really how you want to live.

It's interesting to note that my friend, Jim, along with many high performing people, also schedules several vacations at the start of the new year. By doing this he is making sure that he will "find" the time for his vacations.

## Action step — Planning your time

To be sure that you keep balance in your life, when you are doing your monthly, weekly, or daily plan, have your goals nearby. If you make sure that you regularly plan something in each area — spiritual, health, career, etc., you will be in balance and alignment with your major goals.

In our busy complex society, it is too easy to become caught up in the pace of daily living, only to wake up ten years in the future realizing you're not where you want to be. An investment of a small amount of time, monthly, weekly and daily, to plan your activities will help you achieve more of what you want in your life.

## Wake up and smell the money

Many of what we know today as successful enterprises were actually born out of frustration and need. Opportunities are all around us, all we need to do is begin to pay attention to our surroundings. What do people around you seem to want that they are not getting?

In 1980, Gerald Aul, Pat Senn, and Robert Diaz began observing that people were frustrated at the lack of services being provided by the Post Office and asked, "Why can't people just come in and have merchandise packed and shipped without having to do it all themselves?" This simple question, combined with the frustration they and others were experiencing, led to the start of Mail Boxes, Etcetera. At last count the company, now part of UPS, has more than 3,300 locations worldwide.

Another successful global company, born out of a simple need, is the Honda Corporation. In the years following World War II, with gasoline in short supply, most Japanese were using bicycles as their main form of transportation. Wanting to make it easier for his countrymen to move around, Soichiro Honda invented a small engine that attached to the bicycle enabling it to go faster while still conserving fuel. This little engine was the beginning of Honda.

Barney, the big, loveable, purple dinosaur, who entertains children all over the world, was developed because its creator was not able to find video programs that she felt were suitable for her young child.

What are the opportunities that surround you? One way to uncover these is to pay attention to what people are saying. What do people seem to want that is not available?

If you are a part of your local business community, what opportunities are right in front of you? For example, if you hear several people talking about how they need an Internet site and you know someone who designs Web sites, you might ask for a small referral fee for introducing the Web design company to a new client. You could even act as a free agent, representing one or more local services businesses. If you pay attention, there are always simple, ethical, legal ways you can increase your income in your spare time, especially in today's global business environment.

Many retired executives are able to leverage their business contacts and act as "rainmakers" for a company. Basically, a rainmaker is the person who opens the door for a client company, being paid a referral fee for doing so.

Rainmakers, by the way, are generally among the highest paid people in any company because they bring in the business that generates revenue from the company's products and services.

A friend of mine once received a check that was more than fifty thousand dollars as his "finder's fee." He had simply made an introduction to a key executive for another company's account team.

## Success leaves clues

If you want to become more successful in any area of your life, make a habit of studying successful people. In addition to the ideas, tools, and techniques discussed in this book, libraries and bookstores are filled with wonderful books as well as audio programs to help you along your path.

Make a habit of reading inspiring books and listening to audio programs. Attend live events and tele-seminars whenever possible. Not only will you expand your mind, but you will be in a position to meet and get to know like-minded people. Remember what I said earlier about hanging out with the winners. Develop relationships with other positive people who, like you, want the best life they are capable of achieving.

Make it a practice to read biographies of people you admire and people who have excelled in their life. In doing this you will begin to see the patterns and gain insight as to what these people did to succeed.

If succeeding in business is something that interests you, read biographies of people like Benjamin Franklin; Sam

Walton, founder of Wal-Mart; Bill Gates, founder of Microsoft; Sakichi Toyota, founder of Toyota; Akio Morita, founder of Sony; Ray Kroc founder of McDonald's; Coco Chanel, founder of Chanel; Thomas Edison, inventor of the light bulb; Henry Ford, founder of the Ford Motor Company; Mary-Kay Ash founder of Mary-Kay Company; and other successful business people. In their biographies you will learn what steps they took, how they thought, and most important of all, you will read about the adversity they overcame to reach their goals.

You will learn that no matter what happened, each of these highly successful people persevered until they succeeded. Giving up was never an issue. Failure was viewed as a temporary set back and learning experience.

## On-going personal development

The Japanese have a word, *Kaizen*, which means making small daily improvements in every area of your life. It is a combination of principles taught to them by the late W. Edwards Deming and others, following World War II.

Since we have no word for this in English, I have chosen OPD, *On-going Personal Development* as a reminder to follow this formula for success.

It is not so much what you do once in a while that makes the difference; it is what you do daily. This applies to success in much the same way it applies to health and fitness.

If you want to succeed and grow, make a daily habit of

reading and listening to self-help and inspirational books and audio programs. As little as ten to fifteen minutes a day can make a major difference.

For one thing, if you do this first thing in the morning, you will begin your day on a more positive note, and secondly, you will, over time, have assimilated a lot of powerful, positive and thought provoking material.

One of the great ideas I learned from Jack Canfield, author of *Success Principles* and co-author of *Chicken Soup for the Soul*, is that creativity comes from connecting two ideas that had not previously been connected. By reading and listening to personal development information regularly, you are increasing your capacity for more creative ideas.

# 9

## THE BEST OF YOUR LIFE

Congratulations! You have just completed a major step in making the rest of your life the best of your life. If you've skipped any of the activities, please go back and complete them now.

Within you is the power to change your life and the simple, easy to follow activities in this book have been developed to assist you tapping into that power to create the life you want.

You may want to go back and re-read sections, taking notes along the way. You can use these to remind you of the key points that have helped you. Each time we read something, we understand it a little differently, so re-reading is always a worthwhile activity.

Of course, you'll want to continue your personal development program beyond this book. Making personal growth a life-long endeavor will reward you in untold ways. You can learn more about my other books and programs at www.jim-donovan.com. Be sure to subscribe to my *Jim's Jems* newsletter. It was the beginning of my writing career and I've been publishing it steadily since 1991.

Also, be sure to visit the bonus page, listed on the next page. This is my way of thanking you for reading this book and there is no obligation to download the bonuses there.

Commit now to a steady diet of positive, uplifting information. Devote some time each day to reading books and listening to audio programs that will help you stay on the right track to create your magical life.

Remember the lesson from the timeless James Allen book, *As a Man Thinketh*. In it he says, our minds are like a garden; if we do not plant the seeds of positive ideas, weeds will grow by themselves.

Populate your garden with the seeds of inspiring ideas. Nurture them, act on them, and watch them blossom into the life you were born to live.

You have my sincere best wishes for a joyous, successful, and productive life. May you use your success in an enlightened way, helping to make our world a better place for all.

*Be well and God Bless,*
*Jim Donovan, Bucks County, PA*
*USA*

# BONUS GIFTS FOR YOU

As my way of saying "thank you" for reading this book, I'd like to offer you some additional bonuses. There are no strings attached. Just go to this Web page and obtain your bonuses. While you're there, you will be offered the option of signing up for my *Jim's Jems* newsletter. I urge you to do so since you will continue to receive the type of ideas and information you read here as well as be invited to tele-seminars and more.

**www.bonus.jimdonovan.com**

# ABOUT THE AUTHOR

Jim Donovan, a native New Yorker, has implemented the timeless principles in his books to first turn his own life around, and then to devote his life to helping others do the same. Jim practices these principles every day and is living proof that they work.

A world renowned author and inspiring speaker, he has touched the hearts of thousands of people, just like you, who want a better life. Crossing all ethnic, age, and gender barriers, his simple message has been embraced by people of all ages and all walks of life. From business leaders to single parents, people throughout the world are improving the quality of their lives by following the simple techniques in his books.

Jim has been helping individuals and organizations implement strategies for success for more than 20 years.

Jim became a student of self-help literature in 1986. Seeing the results in his own life, he began writing his newsletter and delivering seminars to help others. This led to his first book and a life dedicated to helping people tap into the power within them and create the life they were born to live.

Jim's practical techniques and powerful stories have made him a sought after speaker for businesses, trade groups and associations. His seminars have benefited audiences nationwide, including banks, medical practices, accounting firms, small business groups, chambers of commerce, women-owned businesses, associations, government employees, network marketing companies, school faculty, and students.

More than just motivating, his seminars *inspire* audiences to take responsibility for their lives, provide them with transformational ideas and strategies for their success, and encourage them to take charge of their destiny and create the life they were born to live.

Jim's programs employ proven techniques that synthesize the most effective information from the forefront of human behavior research. His focus is on helping people produce extraordinary results and make quantum leaps.

**Other books by Jim Donovan:**
*Handbook to a Happier Life*
*This is Your Life, Not a Dress Rehearsal*
*52 Ways to a Happier Life*

Available in book stores or from
www.JimDonovan.com.

To learn more about Jim Donovan's breakthrough seminars and workshops, email jim@jimdonovan.com

Learn how you can use Jim's books in your company, or for any other information, please email Maria@jimdonovan.com.

# RESOURCES

For additional information, ideas, links, and up-to-the-date information, be sure to visit our resource page:

**www.resources.jimdonovan.com**

## Leading Edge Doctors

| | |
|---|---|
| *Ronald Hoffman, M.D.* | www.drhoffman.com |
| *Neil Rosen, O.D.* | www.doctorneilrosen.com |
| *Mark Hyman, M.D* | www.drhyman.com |
| *Stephen Sinatra, M.D.* | www.drsinatra.com |
| *Joseph Mercola, M.D.* | www.mercola.com |
| *Eric Braverman, M.D.* | www.pathmed.com |
| *Russell Blaylock, M.D.* | www.russellblaylockmd.com |
| *Andrew Weil, M.D.* | www.drweil.com |
| *Julian Whitaker, M.D.* | www.drwhitaker.com |
| *Gary Bernard, M.D.* | www.livewwell.com |
| *Jeffrey Dach, M.D.* | www.drdach.com |
| *Phillip Miler, M.D.* | www.anitaging.com |

## Additional medical resources

| | |
|---|---|
| *Life Extension Foundation* | www.lef.org |
| *Advanced Nutrition* | www.advanced-nutrition.com |
| *American College for Advancement in Medicine (ACAM)* | www.acamnet.org |
| *American Academy of Anti-Aging Medicine (A4M)* | www.worldhealth.net |

## Additional resources

| | |
|---|---|
| *Reiki method* | www.reiki.org |
| *EFT* | www.emofree.com |
| *Monika Kovacs* | www.monikakovacs.com |
| *Alex's Lemonade Stand* | www.alexslemonade.org |
| *Twilight Wish* | www.twilightwishfoundation.org |
| *Debtors Anonymous* | www.debtorsanonymous.org |
| *Gamblers Anon.* | www.gamblersanonymous,org |

## Suggested reading for health information

*Life Extension Revolution*, Philip Lee Miller, M.D. and the Life Extension Foundation with Monica Reinagel, Bantam Books 2005.

*Intelligent Medicine*, Ronald L. Hoffman, M.D., Simon & Schuster 1997.

*The UltraMind Solution*, Mark Hyman, M.D., Scribner division of Simon & Schuster 2009.

*The Better Brain Book*, David Perlmutter, M.D. and Carol Colman, The Penguin Group 2004.

*The Sexy Years*, Suzanne Somers, Crown Publishers 2004

*Ageless*, The Naked Truth About Bioidentical Hormones Suzanne Somers, Crown Publishers 2006.

*Breakthrough*, Eight Steps to Wellness, Suzanne Somers, Crown Publishers 2008.

*Prescription for Nutritional Healing*, James Balch, M.D. and Phyliss Balch, C.N.C., Avery Publishing Group

*Owing to the vibratory power of words, whatever man
voices, he begins to attract"*
FLORENCE SCOVEL SHINN (1925)

# FURTHER READING

Below is just a small sampling of the books that I have personally found helpful in my quest for a healthier, wealthier, and happier life. You can find links for these and more on our resource page.

| | |
|---|---|
| *You Can Heal Your Life* | Louise Hay |
| *The Success Principles* | Jack Canfield |
| *Excuses Begone* | Dr. Wayne Dyer |
| *The Courage to Be Rich* | Suze Orman |
| *Start Late, Finish Rich* | David Bach |
| *Millionaire Course* | Marc Allen |
| *Love is Letting Go of Fear* | Gerald Jampolosky |
| *The Secret* | Rhonda Byrne |
| *The Feel Good Guide to Prosperity* | Eva Gregory |
| *Breaking the Rules* | Kurt Wright |
| *Retire Young, Retire Rich* | Robert Kiyosaki |
| *Open Your Mind to Prosperity* | Catherine Ponder |
| *Ask and It Is Given* | Jerry & Esther Hicks |

| | |
|---|---|
| *The Attractor Factor* | Joe Vitale |
| *You Were Born Rich* | Bob Proctor |
| *Power Vs. Force* | David Hawkins, Ph.D. |
| *The Aladdin Factor* | Jack Canfield & Mark Victor Hansen |
| *Awaken the Giant Within* | Anthony Robbins |
| *The Greatest Miracle in the World* | Og Mandino |

## Timeless Classics

| | |
|---|---|
| *The Bible* | |
| *A Course in Miracles* | Foundation for Inner Peace |
| *The Abundance Book* | John R. Price (1987) |
| *Creative Visualization* | Shakti Gawain (2002) |
| *Think and Grow Rich* | Napoleon Hill (1937) |
| *As a Man Thinketh* | James Allen (1900's) |
| *Prosperity* | Charles Fillmore (Unity 1936) |
| *Magic of Believing* | Claude Bristol (1948) |
| *The Game of Life* | Florence Scovel Shinn (1925) |
| *The Science of Getting Rich* | Wallace Wattles (1910) |
| *Lazy Man's Way to Riches* | Joe Karbo (1973) |
| *Moneylove* | Jerry Gillies (1978) |

LaVergne, TN USA
05 April 2010
178273LV00001B/6/P